# Contents

# Seminar Studies in History
Founding Editor: Patrick Richardson

## Introduction

The Seminar Studies series was conceived by Patrick Richardson, whose experience of teaching history persuaded him of the need for something more substantial than a textbook chapter but less formidable than the specialised full-length academic work. He was also convinced that such studies, although limited in length, should provide an up-to-date authoritative introduction to the topic under discussion as well as a selection of relevant documents and a comprehensive bibliography.

Patrick Richardson died in 1979, but by that time the Seminar Studies series was firmly established, and it continues to fulfil the role he intended for it. This book, like others in the series, is therefore a living tribute to a gifted and original teacher.

*Note on the System of References:*
A bold number in round brackets (**5**) in the text refers the reader to the corresponding entry in the Bibliography section at the end of the book. If a name follows the bold number, this is an author of a particular essay in a collection. A bold number in square brackets, preceded by 'doc.' [**doc. 6**] refers the reader to the corresponding item in the section of Documents, which follows the main text. Terms which appear in the Glossary are indicated thus: * the first time they appear.

# Acknowledgements

The author wishes to thank Albert Goodwin and Norman Hampson for introducing him, many years ago, to Revolutionary studies. Thanks are also owed to Roger Lockyer for invaluable and painstaking editorial advice, as well as to the *gardiens* of the *Parc Charruyer* in La Rochelle and the *Jardin des Plantes* in Nantes for providing a pleasant reading environment. Here it proved possible to escape, at long last, from the shadows of Aulard, Jaurès, Mathiez and Lefebvre, with their belief that *liberté* could be sanctified by bloodshed; and equally from the Romantic, but ultimately poisonous, doctrine, derived from Rousseau, that the creation of an omnipotent centralised state and a community of fraternal free citizens were ultimately reconcilable. The author has also been influenced, perhaps more than he should have been in the context of this book, by the brilliant writings of Ian Kershaw on the Third Reich. Thanks are also due to Mrs H. Scott for the typing of this manuscript.

We are grateful to Ginn & Company Limited for an extract from *The Press in the French Revolution* (1971) by J. Gilchrist and W. J. Murray.

For Leslee

# Part One: Introduction

. . . but men's behaviour depends upon a great variety of factors, and that is why history is the most difficult and least advanced of the scientific disciplines.

Georges Lefebvre, *Sur la Loi du 22 Prairial An II*, 1951.

A revolution is a very interesting thing to read about in history, and even to watch, provided that one can keep one's distance; close-up, one is revolted by all the injustice, unhappiness and crime that defile it.

Duc de Lévis, September 1791.

One belief, more than any other, is responsible for the slaughter of individuals on the altars of the great historical ideals . . . This is the belief that somewhere, in the past, or in the future, in divine revelation, or in the mind of an individual thinker, in the pronouncements of history or science, or in the simple heart of an uncorrupted good man, there is a final solution. This ancient faith rests on the conviction that all the positive values in which men have believed must, in the end, be compatible, and perhaps even entail one another.

Isaiah Berlin, *Two Concepts of Liberty*, an inaugural lecture delivered before the University of Oxford on 31 October 1958.

# 1 The Problem

No student of modern history can ignore the French Revolution. Like the Renaissance and the reformation, the scientific revolution of the seventeenth century and the period of wars and revolutions between 1914 and 1919, it marks a geological fault in the strata of modern history. Knowledge of it is essential for any understanding of the development of the modern western world. In the words of Sieyès, the chief ideologist of the Third Estate in 1789, the Revolution aimed at 'ideal models of the beautiful and the good', models for subsequent revolutionary movements to emulate.

It was the Revolution which launched the assault on aristocracy, privilege, titles, feudal dues and clericalism. Europe was never the same after 1789, for the Revolution brought about fundamental changes in government, a change in the nature of warfare as well as in its scale, and a challenge to the established hierarchies, institutions and culture of the *ancien régime*\*. The determination of the French revolutionaries, inspired by the writings of Rousseau, to create a new Jerusalem, a 'heaven below', pushed kings, nobles and bishops over to the defensive (**253**; **86**, ch. 3). On 20 September 1792 the French army defeated the Prussians at Valmy. Goethe, present in the Prussian camp, told his dejected companions: 'From this place and from this day commences a new era in the world's history, and you can all say that you were present at its birth'. The threat which the revolution-in-arms presented to the European political and social order made a return to the *ancien régime* impossible in the long run.

Yet the French Revolution is riddled with paradoxes. A concern with individual liberty and the increased participation of the people in government existed alongside the consolidation of the centralised modern state, and the dictatorship of 1793–94. Lip-service was paid to the Rousseauist concept of direct democracy and the sovereignty of the people, but in practice the franchise was restricted and the Constituent Assembly, let alone the more extreme Convention, saw itself, rather than the nation as a whole as the sole repository of the 'general will' and national interest. An initial concern with

2

humanitarianism, exemplified by the abolition of slavery and torture, coexisted with a new tradition of public violence and insurrection which came to involve mass shootings and drownings at the height of the Terror, when human life was regarded as expendable. Enthusiasm for individual political and legal rights was blended with a new emphasis on the rights of property. The slogans of fraternity and universal brotherhood gave way to intense and expansionary nationalism. Before 1792 revolutionaries denounced war as an outmoded stratagem of monarchs and aristocrats: after 1792 conscription for the 'wars of liberty' foreshadowed the ordeal of total war and the reversion to barbarism depicted in Goya's searing war sketches. At the same time, the Revolution retarded French agrarian, industrial and commercial development for over twenty years. Modern capitalist growth, much assisted by the spread of the railway network, dated only from the mid-nineteenth century. Moreover, it was the Revolutionary period itself which saw the origins of socialism, capitalism's prime enemy.

Both the history and the legacy of the French Revolution are plagued by controversy, often acrimonious. Not only was 'debate over the multifarious legacies of the Revolution . . . to tear apart the country's educated elite for over a century', but historians ever since 1789 have remained deeply divided over its nature and significance (**62**, ch. 3). There seems little agreement on what exactly *was* the 'Great French Revolution', itself very much a celebratory creation of the politicians, historians and local officials of the Third Republic during the 1880s. Alfred Cobban, a noted English historian of France, went so far as to question whether there was a revolution in this sense at all (**29**, ch. 5). If there *was* a French Revolution, then just when did it begin and end? What precisely were its causes and consequences? Can it be described as a 'bourgeois* revolution', or, in Lefebvre's view, a 'bourgeois revolution for equality'? Just who benefited from the Revolution? How far was it a disaster for the majority of those who lived through it?

As well as a Revolution, there was a counter-revolution, both inside and outside France. Internally, counter-revolution could range from armed risings intended to overthrow the Revolutionary government, to an attitude of sullen passive hostility. Externally, the counter-revolution took the form of warfare by other European powers aimed at destroying the Revolution and restoring the Bourbon monarchy to its pre-1789 status and power. Supporters of the counter-revolution within France – the bulk of the clergy plus substantial numbers of peasants, businessmen and the very poor over much of the country – were the major victims of Terror and repression. Violence against them deepened their enmity and resentment against the Revolution and all it represented. They got their chance in the 'White Terrors' of 1795 and 1815 when supporters of the Revolutionary and Napoleonic regimes were hunted down (**142**).

The divisions between Frenchmen at the end of the eighteenth century – for or against the great events of 1789 or 1793–94 – persisted in the nineteenth and twentieth centuries. Revolutions in France in 1830, 1848 and 1870 made the Revolution something of a continuing movement. Fear of a return to the 'anarchic horrors' of 1793, or, alternatively, a desire to re-create the days of liberty, fraternity, democracy and cheap bread remained dominant themes in French public life. Even villages could be split. All too frequently, during the Third Republic, the schoolmaster and the *curé* clung to their rival myths and regarded each other with ill-concealed malevolence (**260**, ch. 7).

As late as the 1940s, the Terror of the Year II* was recalled with dread in parts of the French countryside, as the ghost of Robespierre seemed to walk alongside requisitioning and rationing officials, tax-collectors and anti-clericals. Many of the most vicious and bloody armed clashes between the collaborationist Vichy militia and the Resistance in 1945, as well as the most powerful manifestations of the vengeance of the Left towards their wartime collaborationist enemies in the great 'purge' after 1945, occurred in the very same areas which had witnessed the counter-revolutionary armed risings and the most savage incidence of the Terror in 1792–97 (**260**, ch. 6). If the Revolution inspired Liberals and Republicans in the nineteenth century, then it inspired the Socialist Left in the twentieth. The former tended to look back to the 'liberal' Revolution of 1789–91: the latter to the Revolution of 1793–95 when a revolutionary dictatorship struggled ferociously against war, counter-revolution, and the demands of its own supporters for direct democracy and more economic equality. Only in recent years has the debate on the French Revolution begun to pass from politics into history, though observers of the savage debate between Albert Soboul and François Furet in the 1970s might remain sceptical (**43**).

Some of the questions which have dominated histories of the French Revolution are those which were asked by contemporaries like Barnave and Burke, as well as those who wrote with such passion in the nineteenth century. Was the *ancien régime* so worm-eaten that it virtually collapsed of its own accord, or did it need a good push, making the Revolution 'necessary' and therefore commendable? Was the Revolution as a whole necessary, or did it at some stage 'go wrong' and become 'excessive', acting against the interests of the majority of the people of France? Certainly events in France in the spring of 1789 seemed to offer a prospect of national regeneration that caught the imagination of the whole of Europe, including the young Wordsworth, who declared that 'Bliss was it in that dawn to be alive'. Within two years everything had gone sour; these same men were at each others' throats, while the country was heading for civil war and Terror and some of its former leaders were happy to invade France with foreign armies.

What went wrong? And when did the 'excesses' begin? With the September massacres and declaration of a republic in 1792; the execution of the King in January 1793; the great Terror of 1793–94; or when? Can one, as Cobban asked, still regard the Revolution as a monolithic *bloc*, to be either praised or condemned? How far was the Terror implicit in the ideas and events of 1789 – for example, when Barnave, leader of the pre-Revolutionary riots in Dauphiné, asked whether the blood of those murdered after the capture of the Bastille 'was so pure after all that one should regret its spilling'? Or was it rather something necessarily imposed by the critical circumstances of war, counter-revolution and the impending breakdown of the central government?

Such fundamental questions cannot be fully answered in a short book. Indeed, they will probably never produce final answers, since each generation sees the past through different eyes, and the answers themselves often serve only to provoke further questions. The aims of this book are more modest: firstly to encourage thinking about some of the problems of historical studies raised by the French Revolution; secondly to direct readers to the work of major historians of the Revolution whose writings have been unashamedly plundered in the following pages; and finally, to examine a fraction of the mass of documentary evidence on which historians have based their judgements.

# Part Two: The First French Revolution

## 2 Pre-Revolution, 1787–1789

### The Crisis of the *Ancien Régime*

The French Revolution, which began with the aristocratic revolt of 1787–88 and came to a head in the popular revolt of 1789, can be seen as part of a general movement in the western world. In both Europe and America rulers and sections of the ruled were in conflict. This broad movement can be seen as an 'Atlantic' or 'Democratic' revolution, if one accepts the arguments of Jacques Godechot and R. R. Palmer (**14, 15, 16**). Besides the American Revolution of 1773–83, there were movements all over Europe which aimed at challenging the traditions, privileges, institutions and loyalties of aristocratic society. In Geneva, Holland and England there was growing dissatisfaction with existing forms of social stratification and an increasing unwillingness to tolerate the control of government and public office by privileged and self-recruiting groups.

Compared with the French Revolution, however, these European movements were limited in scope. Conflict tended to be between aristocratic rulers who sought to modernise the machinery of government, and privileged groups who resisted in defence of traditional interests and localised administration (**26**, chs 2 and 9). Everywhere the conflict involved minorities of the population, rather than the urban and peasant masses. In the long run they achieved little, for they resembled a salvo of musket-fire which emitted much noise and smoke, but failed to shake the basic structures of the fortress of established society. Only in France in 1789 did the heavy artillery fire of a popular revolution create a barrage so intense that the fortress crumbled. The French Revolution was more violent, more radical, more prolonged and more democratic than its predecessors. No other revolution involved such widespread participation by the peasants and urban common people. The fact that revolts in Europe were frequent after 1789 and that the Continent was plunged into warfare of a new intensity and scale between 1792 and 1815 bears testimony to the power of the French Revolution as the genuinely explosive element in the European revolutionary mixture (**10**, ch. 2; **15**, vol. ii; **17**).

The demographic, social, economic and ideological pressures which provoked a general crisis of the *ancien régime* in the west were felt most intensely in France, where conflict was endemic from the 1760s (**47**). The French population rose from about 21.5 million in 1700 to over 28 million in 1789, although without a concomitant increase in food supply. Population increase was accompanied by the fragmentation of peasant holdings, virtually no increase in agricultural productivity outside north and north-east France, and poor harvests after 1770. Both wages and employment levels lagged behind the rising price of grain and other basic necessities. Hence substantial sections of the population were faced with a declining standard of living, while in the 1780s the whole country was in the throes of a major economic crisis (**51**; **61**, part II, ch. 2; **114**; **62**, ch. 9). In Strasbourg, for example, rapid population growth meant that by 1789 there was a deficit of 20,000 sacks of grain compared with 1743. The result, as in many other parts of France, was a rising death rate, emigration, and a burgeoning horde of paupers, beggars, vagrants, criminals and prostitutes (**66**; **248**, ch. 1; **246**, ch. 1).

While France's industry managed to keep pace with that of Britain until the 1780s, her agriculture was relatively backward in most areas. The French success story in the eighteenth century was overseas trade: the near-monopoly of trade with the Levant through the Mediterranean, plus the booming Atlantic trade in slaves, sugar and other products of the French Caribbean, which enriched the ports of Bordeaux, Nantes and Le Havre. By contrast, much of the interior was backward, traditionalist and fragmented into isolated local markets. Agrarian production increased, but only because more waste land was put under the plough, rather than through increasing productivity, which was not much more than half that in England. Payment of tithes to the Church and of seigneurial dues to the nobility and bourgeois *seigneurs** weighed heavily in many areas on peasant proprietors and tenants. While peasants owned about a third of the land of France, most holdings were very small and in the poorer and more remote regions away from bourgeois competition. Population pressure and price increases meant an increased rural proletariat, consisting of those who owned no land and who, in bad years, were driven to vagrancy, smuggling and bandit gangs. If nearly all peasants agreed that the burdens on their land – tithes, feudal dues and the bulk of government taxes – were too heavy in a deteriorating economic situation, there remained the fact that rural society was split and plagued with antagonisms in the 1770s and 1780s. Tenant farmers and sharecroppers had little love for the prosperous peasant landowners (*laboreurs* or *gros fermiers*) (**258**, ch. 1). Only peasant proprietors owning large farms in the north and east and parts of the south-west advocated new methods like enclosures and crop rotation. The mass of the peasantry, away from the vicinity of large towns and good communications, opposed such 'agrarian individualism' (**114**; **61**; **46**, ch. 3; **45**, ch. 1).

Not only were French financial institutions primitive, but the manufacturing sector was also structurally backward. Machines, factories and large-scale industrial capital were rare in France. Rural industry was dominated by the domestic system: urban industry by the small workshop. Places like Elbeuf, the wool textile centre of Normandy, which had virtually no nobles and was controlled by an industrial middle class committed to machine and factory production, with 59.7 per cent of its population wage-earners in 1785, were exceptional (**57**, chs 1–2; **82**; **83**). Most towns were either agrarian market towns, great ports, or ecclesiastical and administrative centres. Here, as in the countryside, society was firmly graded. In Toulouse, for example, the twenty richest noble families doubled their income from land in the second half of the century (**55**). The nobility, plus the wealthy mercantile and legal families, owned 75 per cent of the wealth of Toulouse, although they constituted only a small fraction of the population. Yet a quarter of the inhabitants were paupers (**56**).

Similar inequalities existed in Orléans, whose population of 42,000 was dominated by a noble, clerical and rich-bourgeois oligarchy of about 2,600. The 24,000 workers ate inferior bread to that of their betters, even though they spent half their income on it, and wore clothing of cheaper and coarser materials (**54**). In Paris the gap between the very rich minority, the wealthiest of whom were nobles possessing over 500,000 *livres*\*, and the impoverished mass of the people was greater still. The nobility, clergy, upper and middle bourgeois amounted to about 120,000 individuals, while the future *sans culottes* – artisans, small shopkeepers and traders, wage-earners, clerks, journeymen and apprentices – numbered over 500,000. The capital also possessed a large floating population of at least 50,000, seething with large numbers of casual labourers, domestic servants, footloose immigrants, unemployed and criminals (**100**, chs 2–3; **96**, ch. 2). There was, of course, nothing corresponding to the urban working class of modern industrial society. 'Worker' (*ouvrier*) could mean an independent craftsman, a small workshop master, or even a substantial manufacturer, as well as an ordinary wage-earner. The division between masters and men in small-scale industry was inevitably blurred. Nevertheless, neither the French Revolution in general nor the Terror in particular can be understood without some grasp of the permanent underlying antagonism between rich and poor, especially when it is recalled that between 1726–41 and 1785–89 wheat prices increased by 66 per cent, rye by 71 per cent and firewood by 91 per cent, while wages in the building industry rose by only 24 per cent. The harvest failures of 1769–71, 1778–79, 1781–82, 1785–86 and, above all, 1788–89, proved devastating (**24**, ch. 2).

Research and academic debate over the last twenty years have rendered the traditional view of the origins of the French Revolution untenable. The orthodox version was very much a social and economic interpretation, enshrined in books like Lefebvre's *The Coming of the French Revolution*. Marxists like Mathiez, Lefebvre and Soboul believed that the ultimate cause of the Revolution lay in the rise of one particular class, the bourgeoisie*, viewed primarily as the agents and beneficiaries of capitalism. According to the Marxist interpretation, 1789 marked the time when this expanding bourgeois class took power in France and transformed its institutions to their own advantage. Medieval society had been dominated by a landed aristocracy when land was the only major form of wealth. By the eighteenth century, however, economic power had passed largely to the bourgeoisie, buttressed by new forms of wealth based on commerce and industry, as well as a new ideology of progress and reform which promoted increasing resentment of aristocratic privilege. Marxist historians believed that in 1789 the bourgeoisie overthrew the remnants of the aristocratic feudal order, which had still retained political and social dominance despite its economic eclipse, and established a regime dominated by themselves. The triumph of the bourgeoisie was made possible by the collapse of the political authority of the monarchy, unable to pay its way because the aristocracy – the clergy and nobles – clung to their privileges and tax exemptions and used their political leverage to prevent the King and his ministers implementing reforms necessary to restore royal solvency.

Lefebvre acknowledged that the Revolution began in 1787 with a revolt of the aristocracy and higher clergy rather than the bourgeoisie, as part of the aristocratic reaction against the reform schemes of the royal government. But in order to oppose the monarchy more effectively, the nobility recruited support from the bourgeoisie; and the very success of this strategy gave the aspiring bourgeoisie ambitions of their own. In September 1788 they were outraged when the aristocratic *parlement** of Paris declared that the

9

Estates-General would meet in 1789 according to the forms of 1614, with vote by order, so as to ensure that the third estate of commoners would be outvoted by the privileged clerical and noble orders. It was at this stage, according to Marxist orthodoxy, that there began the 'revolt of the bourgeoisie': a class struggle against the privileged orders which culminated in the creation of a National Assembly dominated by the bourgeoisie in June 1789 and in the 'overthrow of feudalism' on 4 August. Thus the way was cleared for the bourgeoisie to put their programme into effect: a programme based on property and wealth rather than birth and hereditary status. The new regime aimed to achieve civil equality by destroying the privileges of the nobility and clergy and creating a society where all men obeyed the same laws, paid taxation on the same basis, enjoyed the same career opportunities and owned property on the same terms.

Yet the bourgeoisie were unable to achieve all this alone. In order to resist the noble-inspired royal attempt to dissolve the National Assembly in June 1789, the bourgeois deputies were obliged to recruit the people of Paris, whose most spectacular achievement was the capture of the Bastille on 14 July. There occurred, therefore, after the aristocratic revolt against the monarchy and the bourgeois conflict with the aristocracy, a third revolt: that of the common people, especially in the capital, based on the economic grievances of the urban workers, particularly high bread prices. Indeed, as Lefebvre pointed out in his *The Great Fear* (1932), there was a fourth revolt, prompted by the unprecedented economic crisis of 1788–89; that of the peasants. This took the form of a nationwide uprising against the feudal dues imposed by noble landlords, and involved peasant risings across France and the widespread burning of *châteaux*. These risings were only damped down when the National Assembly abolished the whole apparatus of 'feudalism' on the night of 4 August 1789 (**62**, part i; **45**, introd.; **258**, ch. 3).

This 'orthodox' version of the Revolution's origins has collapsed under the weight of research and criticism during the last two decades (**81**; **62**, part i). Major criticisms appeared from Alfred Cobban and George V. Taylor who argued that the vast majority of the deputies in the Third Estate (87 per cent) had nothing to do with the world of commerce and industry, being mostly lawyers, government servants and petty office-holders; men who were anything but confident and assured as they saw their incomes depressed during the economic crisis. The bourgeois revolutionaries of 1789 were not hostile to feudalism, since they were property-owners and many of them actually held feudal rights. About 15 per cent of *seign-eurs* were non-noble. Those members of the bourgeoisie who were industrialists, traders and financiers were usually quite uninterested in politics and tended to be hostile to lawyers and officials, who, together with the liberal minority of the nobility, actually spear-headed the Revolution. And far from creating the conditions for un-trammelled capitalism, the Revolution positively retarded capitalist development (**29**, chs 5, 14, 15; **33–37**; **45**; **260**, ch. 9). If the bour-geoisie were not a unified class, neither were the nobility. French nobles were a deeply divided and variegated group, numbering somewhere between 100,000 and 400,000. Between a quarter and a third were of recent origin – families ennobled since 1715. There was considerable antagonism between rich and poor nobles, Court and country nobles; even the Court nobility were split between rival cabals. Moreover, there was a significant minority of nobles who shared the values of the bourgeoisie, while some were prominent in French industry and finance. Their fiscal privileges and exemptions were considerable, although not so much as was once assumed. They were exempt from compulsory billeting, military service, the *corvée* (compulsory road work), the *gabelle* (salt tax) and *taille person-nelle* (a poll tax); but they were obliged to pay the *capitation* (a tax on overall revenues) and the *vingtième* (a 5 per cent tax on net landed revenue). Although their privileges were certainly worth possessing, the French nobility were probably the most highly-taxed in Europe (**78**). Besides, important tax exemptions were also enjoyed by many of the bourgeoisie, especially the commercial magnates, in great mercantile cities like Bordeaux, Nantes and Marseille (**76**; **78**).

Members of the bourgeoisie were constantly purchasing titles of nobility. Even the minority involved in trade and industry were anxious to leave commerce and invest in a landed estate once they had made their fortunes. As the Cambridge historian Tim Blanning has commented: 'With so many bourgeois behaving like nobles and so many nobles behaving like bourgeois, it is difficult to find much evidence of class-conflict between the two' (**45**, part i, ch. 2). In-deed, it is difficult to identify them as separate classes at all. Both groups drew most of their income from landed wealth; both were involved in industrial and commercial investment. To rise from the ranks of the bourgeoisie into the nobility was easy for those with money: 'throughout *ancien régime* society, wealth could overcome al-most any social barrier' (**47**, ch. 2). The real obstacle to 'the career open to talent' was money rather than lack of birth or status. Even those without money did their utmost; Marat, the extreme Jacobin journalist and agitator, falsely claimed to be noble, while before 1789 such eminent Revolutionary leaders as Brissot, Danton, Robespierre and Saint-Just tinkered with their names to make them sound aristocratic.

Given that both the bourgeoisie and the nobility shared a common interest in resisting the royal government, and that there were few qualitative economic differences between them, mutual hostility only became endemic in 1789 for political and social reasons at the end of the major political crisis which commenced in 1786. This crisis was certainly not caused by bourgeois–noble enmity based on economic differences. On the contrary, it has been claimed that after about 1730 there emerged in France a new, relatively unified, social elite of landed proprietors: the *notables*. This elite was to consolidate itself during the Revolution by the abolition of venal offices and noble and clerical privilege, while taking advantage of the marketing of substantial amounts of confiscated Church and *émigré* land (**77**). Neither did there exist an aristocratic dominance of high posts, intensified by an 'aristocratic reaction' and a freezing of social mobility. Many high posts were held by recently-ennobled bourgeois. If some institutions, like the royal army and the *parlement* of Rennes, succeeded in excluding rich *parvenu* nobles, then others, like the *parlement* of Bordeaux, or the great *parlement* of Paris whose jurisdiction covered a third of France, remained wide open to rich men in banking, high finance and government service, most of whom had recently acquired nobility (**95**; **153**; **74**, part i; **75**, ch. 1).

The impact of the Enlightenment is difficult to assess with any precision, but it was certainly not a bourgeois movement. Writers like Montesquieu, Voltaire, Diderot and d'Holbach criticised the Church and virtually every other French institution, yet they were far from being revolutionaries. They aimed at the reform and improvement of institutions rather than their demolition. By the 1760s the *philosophes* of the Enlightenment had become a literary establishment. Their readers also belonged to the social elites of nobles, magistrates, office-holders and lawyers. It was such men in the provinces who read Diderot's *Encyclopédie*, joined the libraries and founded the literary societies, academies and masonic lodges through which the values of the Enlightenment were disseminated (**89**; **90**). They did not anticipate that these values would 'lead to the sort of upheavals that began in 1789 and were to destroy their status, privileges, offices and indeed most of the cultural institutions they patronised' (**47**, part iv, ch. 2).

The ideas of writers like Montesquieu and Rousseau inspired men to seek reform but not revolution – of which, at least in the modern sense of the term, they had no concept. *Philosophes* argued that the principles of human society could be discovered like those of the natural world, and then applied to the regeneration of men and government. Europe, they believed, was approaching a new era of progress and improvement which could bring about the perfectibility of man. Such optimism was an essential ingredient in the 'Revolutionary spirit' after the summer of 1789. Stress was placed, for example, on a new 'natural' hierarchy of property and talent, rather than on traditional birth and privilege, even if this meant disregarding the extent to which talent and property had possessed ample opportunities before 1789. Even the Terror of 1793–94 could be viewed as an attempt to promote human improvement on a rational basis [**doc. 22**].

One major feature of the *ancien régime* was an increase in basic literacy and a rapid expansion of the publishing industry catering for both educated and uneducated readers. The literacy rate for males rose from around 30 per cent in 1650 to around 50 per cent in 1780. Significantly, the most literate areas of France were the north and east, which, together with Protestant enclaves throughout France, provided the most fervent support for the Revolution after 1789. The influence of the Enlightenment reached beyond the social elites, though in distorted fashion and in the face of the fact that south of the river Loire and in parts of Brittany, French as spoken in the east and north-east was not normally used by the common people and was imperfectly understood. The American historian Robert Darnton has uncovered a clandestine industry of Grub Street writers, pirate presses, backroom bookstores, street traders in the towns and book-hawkers (*colporteurs*) in the countryside. Hack writers, resentful of their inability to join the Enlightenment literary elite, wrote titillating accounts of sexual depravity in high society which helped loosen the bonds of deference and plant the ideological seeds of revolution among the common people. The characters depicted in this literature as adulterous, promiscuous, incestuous and homosexual were invariably members of the 'privileged orders'. Political radicalism was implicit in libels on the royal family. The corpulent and lazy Louis XVI was portrayed as an impotent cuckold, while Marie Antoinette was described as an insatiable bisexual nymphomaniac who had infected most members of the Court with venereal disease. Such pornography appears to have made a deep impression on the common people's image of the privileged orders, especially the Court. The undeserved reputation for depravity of

Marie Antoinette ('the Austrian whore') persisted until her trial – when she was accused of incest with her eight-year old son as well as treason – and even beyond, to her public execution, at which obscene libels about her sold like hot cakes (**62**, part ii; **93**; **91**; **92**, ch. 4).

Although the *philosophes* were integrated into elite society, they remained highly critical of, as well as alienated from, the royal government, and their writings proved more radical in their impact than they had perhaps intended. Liberal nobles and the professional middle classes clearly sought inspiration in these writings. The French *parlements*, in their clash with the royal government in the 1760s and 1780s, invoked Montesquieu's belief in the need for 'intermediary bodies' as a buffer between monarch and subjects. They also pillaged the works of Rousseau, whose *Social Contract* (1762) developed the theory leading to the concepts of the 'sovereignty of the people' and 'the general will': the idea that society as a whole should decide its best interests, ideally by means of direct democracy. Rousseau's emphasis on the individual and on the equality of men as moral agents had strong democratic implications (**26**, chs 1 and 2; **85**, ch. 8; **86**, chs 1 and 3; **94**).

Conflict between monarch and *parlements* in the 1760s over royal administration and taxation resulted in the use by *parlementaires* of a good deal of potentially revolutionary language. Words like 'citizen', 'motherland' (*la patrie*), 'constitution', 'nation', 'rights of the nation' and 'demands of the nation' were used so often that they virtually became revolutionary slogans in themselves (**14**, vol. i, ch. 14; **75**, ch. 6). The realisation that the political ideas of the *philosophes* could be put into practice was deepened by the American Revolution, which appeared to radical Europeans a new enlightened experiment leading to a just society where men were freed from the stultifying legacy of the past. Institutions, it was thought, should be judged by their utility, not by their antiquity or sacredness (**16**, part ii, ch. 3).

The *parlements* and the provincial estates were not the only source of disturbance during the reign of Louis XVI. A tradition of revolt over bread prices and wages went back to at least the early 1770s (**96**; **97**, chs 3–7). Arthur Young, the English agricultural expert who travelled in France in the late 1780s, wrote: 'The deficit would not have produced the Revolution but in concurrence with the price of bread'. Workers spent something like half their income on bread in normal times, but up to 58 per cent in times of economic crisis and a disastrous 88–90 per cent in the near famine conditions of the midsummer of 1789 (**98**). Government awareness that high bread prices invariably led to food riots and popular disturbances resulted in ministerial steps to ensure the provisioning of urban markets. Yet riots still took place (**100**, ch. 3; **66**). In 1774 there was the large-scale 'Flour War' (*guerre des farines*) in the Paris region, followed by food riots at Toulouse and Grenoble in 1778 and Rennes in 1785, as well as protests in 1785 and 1786 against the *octrois*, the ring of customs posts recently erected around Paris. Strikes for higher wages and demonstrations against inflated prices of basic consumer goods were also frequent. By 1789 over 18,000 workers in Lyon depended on public charity (**67**).

As yet these popular movements were limited in their aims to economically basic questions of wages, prices and working conditions. None of them involved the kind of coherent criticism of the *ancien régime* developed by the liberal nobility and professional bourgeoisie from the ideas of the *philosophes*, at least until links were made with the popular movement in the winter of 1788–89. Yet a potential broadly-based movement was coming into being. Distorted information, exaggerated rumours, songs, pictures and theatre and puppet shows played on popular fears, especially the overriding one of famine, and led to a search for an individual, group, or institutional scapegoat. These phenomena were to prove a constant factor in the Revolution, certainly until December 1794. If 'aristocrats' and the royal government could be substituted for the traditionally-hated miller, baker and food-hoarder as 'enemies of the people', then the step from a food or wage riot to aggressive and violent revolutionary action was not a long one (**101**). In 1788 the 'aristocratic revolt' began a movement which brought together dissident nobles, discontented bourgeois and popular unrest with some common aims and common enemies. The outcome was the dramatic events of 1789 (**80**).

## The Aristocratic Revolt

The immediate cause of the French Revolution was the financial crisis which led to a clash between the government and the nobility in 1787 and 1788. Calonne, Controller-General of Finances since 1783, informed the King in August 1786 that an annual deficit of 112 million *livres* existed on a total revenue of 475 million. Since 1776, 1,250 million had been borrowed, while the four wars waged between 1733 and 1783 had cost 4,000 million (**79**). The third *vingtième* was soon to expire and government credit was exhausted.

Credit was twice as expensive in France as in England and even at prohibitive interest rates it was proving difficult for the government to borrow further sums. Drastic economies in Court and government expenditure would save only 30 per cent of total expenses at the very most. Radical reform therefore seemed the only alternative to bankruptcy and the total collapse of the royal government. Raising indirect taxes on consumer goods was hardly practicable, as France was already very heavily, if inefficiently, taxed. There would have to be increased revenue from direct taxation, involving reduction of the fiscal exemptions of the nobility, clergy and wealthier bourgeoisie (**63**, chs 1 and 3; **62**, part ii, ch. 1). Such reforms implied changes in the chaotic French administration so fundamental as to amount to a virtual revolution. Not that there was really a genuine possibility of pushing through such reforms, for that would require more power than the French monarchy, absolute only in theory, possessed. Behind the impressive surface of professional ministers, provincial *intendants**, governors and military commanders, there lay bewildering disorder. There was no central treasury where accounts were kept, revenue taken in and payments made; nor any genuine notion of an annual budget. Most of the state's finances were handled by independent financiers who creamed off a good deal before the money reached Versailles. Sometimes they even lent the King his own money so that he could meet their interest charges. Not only were the internal administrative units of the country confused and overlapping but royal power was subject to political checks from the organised Church, *parlements* and provincial estates, as well as from entrenched municipal rights and exemptions. Poor communications, made no better by a mass of tolls and barriers, were a further hindrance to efficient administration from the centre (**62**, part ii, ch. 2).

In February 1787 the government decided to summon an Assembly of Notables. This body, allegedly handpicked for docility, was presented with a reform programme which included a new graduated land tax. This was set as a percentage of the crop to make it inflation-proof, and had to be paid in kind, in order to limit evasion. It was widely recognised at the time that Louis XVI, by reviving an institution that had been in abeyance since its last meeting in 1626, was implicitly acknowledging that the existing political system could no longer cope with the demands being made upon it. When the Assembly met, there was agreement among all except the clerical members that fiscal privileges should be abolished. Many of them believed that it was Calonne who, by his lavish spending and general mismanagement, had brought about the crisis, and they were well aware that his proposals, as they stood, would have the effect of freeing the crown finances from any kind of control. The government also had its opponents within the Court itself. One group took its lead from Cardinal de Brienne, Archbishop of Toulouse, who hoped to drive Calonne from office and take his place. Another group was led by Necker, a former Controller-General, who claimed that he had been telling the truth when he said he had balanced the budget, including war expenditure, during his first ministry. If France were in fact solvent in 1781, as one historian claims, then the fiscal crisis was indeed the product of avoidable mismanagement (**261**).

In the event, Calonne's plans were rejected, and the King dismissed him in April 1787, replacing him with Brienne. Yet Brienne's proposals for a modified land tax and minor concessions on the part of the crown were in turn rejected by the Assembly, in favour of a loan and the prolongation of existing taxation. Even before the King dismissed Brienne in May, some of the young lawyers among the Notables were arguing that a drastic reform package, if it were to succeed, would require the assent of a 'truly national assembly'. Such a body, it was claimed, already existed in the form of the Estates-General, a gathering of the traditional three orders – clergy, nobility and commoners – which had not met since 1614 (**63**, chs 1–3; **68**; **70**).

The first Assembly of the Notables marked the real beginning of the political crisis which culminated in the French Revolution. The elites of the Notables, *parlements* and provincial estates, while often at loggerheads with each other, agreed in their unwillingness to accept any strengthening of the royal government. Without the support of the Notables, *parlements* and provincial estates, the monarchy was unable to obtain the confidence of bankers in Amsterdam and elsewhere and obtain substantial loans. It was now apparent that financial reform was inextricably linked to major administrative reform, amounting to a fundamental overhaul of French institutions. As Barnave pointed out, the crown must either become a military despotism and destroy ancient institutions and privileges by force; or it must transform itself into some sort of constitutional monarchy. The tragedy for Louis XVI and his ministers was that neither alternative was really practicable, if only because the King himself was devoid of self-confidence and resolution (**100**, ch. 5; **49**, ch. 4; **18**, ch. 2).

Some attempt was made at a policy of force, which immediately led to what has been termed 'the noble revolt'. In July 1787 Brienne tried and failed to persuade the *parlement* of Paris to accept the reforms rejected by the Notables. The *parlements* – law courts rather than 'Parliaments' with legislative powers – again put forward their long-standing claims to register royal decrees and to protest against 'unconstitutional' government legislation, claims aimed at thwarting 'royal absolutism' which had brought head-on clashes with the royal government in the 1760s and 1770s. The conflict of 1787 was but another stage in a long war of attrition between the *parlements* and the King's ministers (**73**; **75**). In challenging the royal administration by scuttling financial reform, the *parlements* posed as the defenders of popular 'rights' and 'liberties'. The more reckless *parlementaires* espoused a constitutional radicalism which dangerously approached a revolutionary stance.

When the Paris *parlement* rejected Brienne's reforms as 'contrary to the rights of the nation', it was exiled to Troyes, although its obstinacy was endorsed by most of the other *parlements* and by street demonstrations of young law clerks and porters in Paris (**63**, chs 4–6; **19**, ch. 1). Brienne evaded reiterated demands for the calling of the Estates-General, and recalled the *parlement* of Paris in September 1787 amid anti-government riots, followed by further demonstrations in which bourgeois citizens and members of the legal profession were joined by journeymen. Thus the *menu peuple** of the capital were drawn into political rioting for the first time, although the *parlementaires* themselves strongly disapproved of disorder in the streets (**96**, ch. 3; **69**). Tracts and pamphlets persuaded many of the demonstrators that the aristocratic *parlements* were defending popular rights and established custom against 'despotism' (**72**). Furthermore, the weakness of the forces of order in Paris was clearly revealed – something the crowd was to remember in April and July 1789.

When the *parlement* still refused to accept new taxes and on 19 November reiterated its demand for the calling of the Estates-General, a renewed battle between the *parlements* and the monarchy began which lasted six months, deepening the financial crisis, robbing the government of its reforming zeal and spreading defiance of the monarchy more widely among the educated nobility and bourgeoisie (**100**, ch. 5). Again the government resorted to force. Leading *parlementaires* were arrested in May 1788 and the *parlements* themselves deprived of many of their powers. The consequence was outbursts of disorder in various parts of the country; opposition to the government was stiffened by the effects of unemployment and high commodity prices after the ruinous harvest of 1788. Royal judges and officials were mobbed in Paris and Toulouse; the aristocracy of Franche-Comté demanded restoration of the province's defunct Estates; there were riots against the *intendant* in Brittany and a popular rising against royal troops in Dauphiné. In the latter region the liberal nobility and the leading bourgeoisie came together to demand the end of fiscal privileges and the entry of commoners to all offices (**63**; **64**; **62**, part ii, ch. 8; **25**, ch. 2; **71**).

Faced by the united opposition of the judicial, clerical and lay nobility as well as by a breakdown of royal authority in the provinces, the government, whose capacity to borrow money was now exhausted, was obliged to surrender. Brienne was succeeded by Necker and on 8 August it was agreed that the Estates-General should meet at Versailles on 1 May 1789. Although there were street demonstrations when the King reinstated the *parlements* on 23 September, popular enthusiasm for the latter soon evaporated when the Paris *parlement* stipulated that the Estates-General should be convoked according to the forms of 1614: that is, an equal number of representatives for each order and the three orders to vote separately. Thus the clergy and nobility would be able to impose their combined will on the commoner Third Estate and retain their privileges. In June a new 'patriot party' had begun to emerge, composed of *philosophes*, liberal nobles, lawyers and magistrates. After September it was no longer willing to support the *parlement* in its opposition to the commoners, for the *parlementaires* wilfully ignored the political and social ambitions of bourgeois members of the professions and the desire of many 'patriots' to see the end of 'privilege' and 'feudalism'. During the autumn and winter of 1788 there took place a realignment of radical forces. What had been a clash between the monarchy and the aristocracy, the latter being supported by many commoner groups, now tended to become a broad conflict between the privileged and the unprivileged. Many of the unprivileged, largely the educated bourgeoisie, began to argue that the privileged orders had only opposed the government for fear of being made to shoulder their fair burden of taxation. The monarchical and aristocratic antagonists of 1787–88 were apparently to be pushed together in 1789 to face the challenge of the Third Estate. In practice, matters were not quite so clear-cut, for the commoners proved able to find allies among the liberal nobility, sections of the higher and lower clergy and some progressive magistrates.

Before the end of 1788 the patriot party, organised in clubs, societies and corresponding committees, was making the running by putting forward the key ideas which were to dominate the thinking of the Third Estate in the spring and summer of 1789: the desirability of a declaration of rights, the idea of 'national sovereignty' and the need for a constitution. Especially influential was the Parisian 'Society of Thirty', composed of a cross-section of the capital's social and intellectual elite: magistrates, priests, courtiers, bankers, academicians, lawyers and journalists. It launched a campaign of agitation and pamphlets aimed at the bourgeoisie, demanding no voting by order and double representation for the commoners in the Estates-General. With its condemnation of legal distinctions between citizens, the Society sought to stir bourgeois resentment against the privileged orders (**111**). Over 2,500 pamphlets were circulated in late 1788 and early 1789, posing a direct challenge to traditional hierarchy and the privileged structure of French society.

The immediate issue, however, was the convocation of the Estates-General. How many deputies should be elected for each order? How would they vote? Partly because of pressure of public opinion, partly to punish the nobility for their institutional opposition to the royal government, the King and Necker accepted the principle of double representation for the Third Estate. The more contentious issue of voting by order or by head was postponed until the actual meeting of the Estates-General. In the meantime, the King and his ministers sat back to await events, leaving the country more or less without central government (**18**, ch. 3; **25**, ch. 2).

It was in the debates over the composition of the Estates-General that the highly-educated professional bourgeoisie began to become conscious of their own separate identity and values. Although a section of the bourgeoisie had attacked rationalist Enlightenment ideas, the bulk of them now followed the enlightened nobility in becoming increasingly aware of the importance of national affairs. Until August 1788 the bourgeoisie had supported the liberal nobles in their struggle against 'despotism' and the belief that liberal representative institutions were necessary if the men of property who bore the bulk of direct taxation were to have any say in how the money was spent (**62**, ch. 7). But the increasingly hostile attitude of conservative nobles in the winter of 1788–89 led the bourgeoisie for the first time to realise that they had interests of their own.

The events of 1789 must be considered against a background of intense economic crisis, a result of the catastrophic harvest of 1788, which had been preceded by a drought and storms. Bread prices consequently rose to starvation levels and provoked widespread unrest, including attacks on granaries, popular price-fixing of bread (*taxation populaire\**) and riots against farmers, bakers, corn dealers, gamekeepers and tax collectors. Ancillary causes of distress and disturbance were the slump in the wine trade and the flood of cheap English manufactures into France after the Anglo-French trade treaty of 1786 (**98**; **101**; **72**, ch. 9). So far as the common people were concerned, the government was to blame rather than the weather or English industrial enterprise. Unemployed workers blamed it for concluding the treaty with England, or suspected it of being in league with grain hoarders and speculators in a deliberate policy of starving the people: the *pacte de famine* which played so large a part in popular demonology. Widespread hunger also led to exceptionally violent opposition to government taxation, especially the indirect taxes on food and drink, as well as to the tolls and duties levied on most food products. In such circumstances, the exemptions of the rich were more than ever resented. It was in this disturbed context that news of the convocation of the Estates-General led many of the common people to expect prompt, comprehensive action to solve their problems once the deputies reached Versailles in May 1789.

## Elections

By the beginning of 1789 there existed a new consciousness of social divisions. This was partly a result of the flood of propaganda pamphlets during the previous six months, partly because a Second Assembly of Notables rejected doubling the number of Third Estate deputies on 6 November, provoking popular wrath, and partly because the more conservative members of the clergy and nobility were pushed by the noisy campaigning into a more intransigent defence of their legal status and privileges. In January 1789 the Abbé Sieyès, the leading ideologue of the progressive groups, published the most celebrated pamphlet of the Revolution: 'What is the Third Estate?' So long as the clergy and the nobiltity refused to share common rights and obligations with their fellow citizens, he argued, they did not constitute a valid section of the nation and should therefore enjoy no rights at all. In the meantime, the Third Estate deputies were the sole true representatives of the nation (**105**, chs 1–2).

Although the electoral arrangements for the Estates-General were complex, basically each electoral district was to choose deputies for all three orders, with each order deliberating separately and selecting its own deputies. Because the Third Estate was far too numerous, under conditions of virtual manhood suffrage, to elect deputies directly, they elected them indirectly in two stages. Their premier task was to elect regional assemblies, who were to vote for the actual choice of deputy for the region. These regional, or electoral, assemblies were authorised to draw up *cahiers*\* – lists of grievances and proposals for reform to guide the deputies, to be considered eventually by the Estates-General. The majority of the elections were held in March and April 1789, against a background of economic distress, popular unrest and general political excitement, though without any attempt by the government to interfere with the election. Throughout the election period expectation mounted since within each of the three orders the lead was taken by those who sought sweeping reform and no return to the pre-1787 system.

Within the clerical order, the form of election favoured parish *curés* at the expense of 'superior' monks and cathedral canons. The hostility of the *curés* towards the bishops (all nobles) and non-pastoral clergy was reflected in the election of 192 parish priests, nearly all well-educated scions of prosperous urban bourgeois families, against only fifty-one bishops, out of 303 clerical deputies (**104**). Therefore the deputies of the First Estate arrived at Versailles already divided on some issues. At the same time, all ecclesiastics agreed that Catholicism should remain the established religion, retaining control of education, public health and organised charity; they also regarded the toleration of Protestants since 1787 as undesirable at the very least. On the other hand the clergy were willing to surrender their fiscal privilege of self-taxation, under which the Church had been a self-financing, autonomous corporation, exempt from taxes through making 'free gifts' (*dons gratuits*) to the royal exchequer (**103**).

Noble electoral assemblies tended to be equally divided, especially when many recently-ennobled bourgeois were excluded. Court nobles and noble magistrates found it difficult to get elected by provincial poor nobles who were jealous of the educated and loquacious 'superior' courtiers and judges. Yet the noble deputies, most of whom were socially conservative, in the event proved remarkably sympathetic to the claims of the Third Estate. Only 41 per cent of the noble *cahiers* insisted on voting by order, while 89 per cent favoured the loss of fiscal privileges. Fewer than 10 per cent insisted on the preservation of nobility as a distinct legal order.

Elections for the Third Estate, with the franchise wider than for any representative body in Europe, were relatively harmonious. Most electors were, of course, peasants, but the district assemblies which actually elected the deputies were almost exclusively bourgeois. So were the deputies themselves. Not one peasant or artisan deputy was chosen, though some nobles were – notably Mirabeau, to become the most prominent orator in the National

Assembly. Only 13 per cent of the deputies could be classified as businessmen; 10–12 per cent were purely landowners; 25 per cent were lawyers; and 43 per cent were legally-trained government office-holders. This was to be expected, given that lawyers – who were highly educated and skilled in public speaking and drafting official documents – had always been the natural leaders of non-noble Frenchmen (**125**). The deputies were also very urban-based, nearly three-quarters coming from towns with more than 2,000 inhabitants at a time when 80 per cent of the population lived in smaller communities. A quarter of the deputies came from large towns inhabited only by 10 per cent of the population.

The *cahiers* for the Third Estate were not so radical as was once believed. The views of peasants and artisans, expressed in their primary *cahiers* and overwhelmingly demanding the end of seigneurial rights in many parts of France, were often laundered out by the general assemblies [**doc. 1**]. The general *cahiers*, summaries of the primary ones, firmly demanded vote by head at Versailles, equality of taxation, no taxation without consent, careers open to talent and guaranteed civil liberties, but there was no general desire for abolition of seigneurial rights (despite the views of the peasants), or for the end of venal offices and trade guilds, while the mandate for confiscation of Church lands and the abolition of tithes, urban and provincial corporate privileges, monasticism and nobility itself, was relatively weak. Yet most of them were in fact destroyed within a year. What transformed them into radicals and revolutionaries, besides splitting the clergy and embittering the nobility, was not the experience of the *ancien régime*, but the events of May to July 1789 (**62**, ch. 8).

Contemporary observers and many historians since have tended to exaggerate the degree of conflict between the privileged orders and the rest of the nation. All three estates agreed on the need for fiscal equality and for the King to rule by means of a constitution in which executive power would remain with the monarch, while the Estates-General, meeting regularly, would control taxation. Individual rights should be guaranteed by law. Everyone agreed that the Church needed reforming, with increased status for the parish clergy. There was also a consensus on measures to stimulate the economy, such as the abolition of internal customs barriers and the standardisation of weights and measures. All discussions took place in an extraordinary atmosphere of hope and expectation – that the regeneration of France was imminent and would become a model for civilised humanity. The deputies were to be tragically mistaken.

# 3 Liberal Revolution, 1789–1792

*Quatre-Vingt-Neuf*

When the 561 deputies for the first two Estates and the 578 for the Third finally convened at Versailles on 4 May 1789, initial hope and optimism soon gave way to anger and frustration. Louis XVI and his ministers had no programme to present and no lead to offer on major issues. They merely expressed a hope that a new financial system could be constructed and a package of reforms introduced, but avoided the crucial issue of voting by head. Meanwhile the nobility voted to maintain itself as a separate order, as did the clergy, though by a very narrow majority. Third-Estate resentment was much stirred by its members having to wear black, like the *curés*, and to follow in processions behind the splendidly and colourfully costumed nobles and bishops.

After a month of procedural wrangling, the Estates-General had achieved nothing. Yet the Third Estate was sustained by the very fact of meeting separately, as well as by the *cahiers* of the commoners and by the growing newspaper press. The royal government having presented no policies, the field was still open (**100**, ch. 7; **62**, ch. 10; **25**, ch. 3). Hence the Commons, as they began to call themselves, held firm against the King and the intransigent majority of the nobility. Deputies from Brittany and the Dauphinois emerged as leaders and made it clear that the Third Estate was only willing to conduct business in a general assembly with voting by head. So far the nobility had remained aloof, the majority of politically inexperienced country squires being easily manipulated, for the moment, by eloquent Court conservatives. By contrast, the First Estate was seriously divided, with many parish priests and a few bishops ready to join the Third.

In Court circles it was felt that Necker was letting the situation drift, and the King and his ministers now began quietly to reinforce the troops at Versailles. But this was noticed by the crowds who constantly kept arriving from Paris and rumours soon spread of an 'aristocratic plot' to obstruct the work of the Estates-General and provide the King with an excuse for a dissolution. Already the influence of the Paris crowd was being felt. Riots and disorder had abated during the expectant atmosphere of the first few weeks of the meeting of the Estates, but they reappeared when there were no immediate results at Versailles and when further increases in bread prices caused widespread panic.

It was on 10 June that the Third Estate became revolutionary and claimed national sovereignty from the King and his ministers when it embarked on delaying tactics by resolving to verify the credentials of each deputy, after vainly inviting both the First and the Second Estate to join it. This was in direct defiance of the King's orders. Now the question was whether the Third Estate could retain the initiative and make the Revolution a going concern, since over the next few weeks there was bound to be a royal counter-attack. As yet, however, the Third Estate had no fully articulated programme of reform; that was to take another two months.

On 17 June the Third Estate, now joined by a group of clerical deputies, called itself, at the suggestion of Sieyès, the 'National Assembly', with an implicit claim to be a sovereign body with supreme power in the state, able to authorise existing taxation and guarantee the national debt. Louis XVI was no longer sovereign: the deputies in the Third Estate had become revolutionaries (**24**, ch. 1). Such a direct challenge at last spurred the King to action, with the announcement of a 'Royal Session' on 23 June at which he would impose his programme. When the Third Estate found itself locked out of its meeting hall on 20 June after a breakdown in communications, it assembled, outraged and suspicious, in a nearby indoor tennis court, and took an oath not to disperse until a constitution had been drawn up. Two days later a majority of clerical deputies joined the National Assembly. The Royal Session proved the swan song of the *ancien régime*, for while the King offered concessions on no taxation without the consent of the Estates, he capitulated to the conservative and Court nobility by rejecting voting in common by the three Estates. The Commons, now reinforced by some liberal nobles as well as most of the clergy, heard the royal proposals, presented in the form of an ultimatum, in obdurate silence, refusing to move when ordered to do so by the King. The attempt by the crown to give a lead therefore came too late, as the King proved unable to exert his authority. Not only were his ministers at loggerheads, but he still lacked a sufficient concentration of troops at Versailles to dissolve the National Assembly in the face of hostile public opinion. The nobles and clergy now realised that they could expect little in the way of royal support, while their numbers had been weakened by defections to the National Assembly, whose meetings were cheered by crowds whose enthusiasm led them to take the five-hour walk from Paris to Versailles (**22**, book ii, ch. 2; **61**, ch. 5; **62**, ch. 10).

The King's only hope of regaining the initiative and reasserting royal authority lay in the army. There were already 4,000 troops around Paris and on 26 June orders were issued to bring up another 4,800, with a further 11,500 called up on 1 July (**109**, ch. 2). It was no longer possible to doubt the government's intention to dismiss the National Assembly by force. But popular disturbances in Versailles and Paris were daily growing more violent. Moreover the 3,600 French Guards who formed the core of the Paris garrison and acted as a police force were no longer proving reliable, as many units passed resolutions not to obey their officers. So Louis XVI had to play for time while substantial troop reinforcements marched towards Paris. On 27 June he ordered the rump of the clerical Estate and the separatist nobles to join the National Assembly, thereby making it genuinely 'National', with vote by head and no separate orders. This apparent transfer of sovereign power to the Assembly caused celebrations in Paris and firework displays at Versailles. Yet the Assembly was aware of the troop movements. It had no soldiers of its own and could therefore be saved only by the people of Paris, a city of 650,000 and six times larger than the biggest provincial towns.

There seemed a good chance of salvation from this source, for popular disturbances in the spring of 1789 owed something to exasperation with the stalemate at Versailles. Substantial sections of the French population, as well as the Third-Estate deputies, believed that the King would try to disperse the National Assembly. The nobility, it was rumoured, led by Artois, the King's brother, were plotting to overthrow the Assembly and seize power; the 'plotters' were said to be in league with grain speculators and hoarders in a 'famine pact' to starve the people into submission. Increasing numbers of brigands, a consequence of poverty and unemployment, were regarded as the shock troops of the 'plotters', ready to lay waste the countryside at the appropriate signal [**doc. 15**]. Fear was present everywhere: fear of people from the neighbouring village or from across the river; fear of people in a different social group, as when the *château* de Quincey near Vesoul in Franche-Comté accidentally blew up during a village celebration – an occurrence which was interpreted as the start of a deliberate campaign by the nobility to exterminate the Third Estate (**113**, part ii, ch. 1). Many of the hundreds of 'loyal addresses' sent to Versailles warned the deputies to be on their guard against a sudden show of force by the King and the nobility. The cellars of the palace of Versailles, it was rumoured, were already mined (**61**, ch. 6; **180**, ch. 7; **62**, ch. 12).

As a consequence of fear and rumour, the people began to arm, forming local militias or 'peasant guards' for defence against 'brigands'. By early July a substantial area of France was under arms, ready to stand by the Assembly if the King attempted to dissolve it. In reality, the troops available to the King were much less numerous and reliable than popular imagination believed. Moreover, Louis was now aware of the possibility of civil war and was anxious to avoid it. Troops were seduced by popular revolutionary propaganda and exhausted by constant police activity against rioters. Fragmentation of units into small detachments to deal with scattered disturbances seriously weakened the chain of command. Many soldiers themselves shared the antagonism of the people towards the privileged orders. If the King were persuaded to attempt a show of force in a desperate last-minute attempt to save the *ancien régime*, then a dispersed, disorganised and unreliable army would be faced by a vast Parisian crowd of armed and enthusiastic people in an almost permanent state of insurrection (**100**, ch. 7; **69**; **106**; **109**, ch. 2; **112**).

Such an attempt was made from 26 June onwards, when the King issued a series of marching orders summoning troops. By 4 July there were 30,000 soldiers in the Paris area, the King refusing requests from an alarmed National Assembly that they be removed. The inevitable clash came when Louis XVI dismissed the 'liberal' Necker on 11 July without having clear plans what to do next. Such indecision allowed the pamphleteers, hack journalists and mob orators like Danton to have a field day under the aegis of the Duc d'Orléans in the cafés at his Palais Royal, outside the jurisdiction of the Paris police. It was they, as well as the 407 electors of the Paris Third Estate at the Hôtel de Ville, who encouraged the *menu peuple* of Paris to rise and take the initiative (**25**, ch. 3; **62**, ch 11). News of Necker's dismissal prompted the risings which led to the fall of the Bastille and collapse of the *ancien régime*, risings which were partly food riots, but which also aimed at forestalling a dissolution of the National Assembly and an armed *coup* against the capital.

On Sunday 12 July crowds gathered at the Palais Royal, clashed with dragoons and occupied the Tuileries palace. Throughout the night of 12–13 July the tocsin (alarm bell) rang and the crowd combed the city for arms. Attention was then turned to the fifty-four customs posts (*barrières*) erected in 1785 to levy duty on goods entering the capital, which had increased the price of foodstuffs and firewood in Paris. Forty of these were set ablaze and the ten-foot wall around the city demolished in places. Prisons were attacked, especially those suspected of containing grain or arms. Order in Paris had broken down.

What transformed a riot into an insurrection was the reaction of the Paris electors, the bourgeois representatives of the sixty electoral districts who had chosen the deputies for the Third Estate. Since then they had continued to meet informally and on 13 July they seized the initiative, organizing 48,000 National Guards*, partly to control the popular movement, despite being explicitly forbidden by the King to form the Guard. The electors and the city council possessed sufficient influence to guide what was still basically a spontaneous movement and turn it into a controlled and disciplined insurrection in a situation where Paris was ringed by royal troops. Muskets which had been looted from gunsmiths' shops on the previous day were distributed to the National Guard. The governor of the *Invalides* was persuaded to part with 28,000 more, plus twenty cannon. An urgent need for 350 barrels of gunpowder and supplies of musket-balls prompted a march by 8,000 men on the Bastille, a medieval fortress-prison which dominated the working-class areas of the east-end of Paris. But the governor resisted and the crowd broke in after persuading a hundred highly-professional French Guards, an elite, if rather undisciplined, regiment, responsible for garrisoning Paris, to bring up cannon. About a hundred of the attackers were killed, while the governor, his deputy and the former head of the municipal government were decapitated and their heads paraded on pikes.

The great *journée*\* of 14 July ended in a major victory with the capture of a potent symbol of 'royal despotism'. Troops had been withdrawn from the streets to the parade-ground of the Champ de Mars; 1,500 Paris police remained inactive because of lack of government support and direction (**109**). The capital was not attacked and the crowd, perhaps deterred by the National Guard, did not turn to looting. Control of the city passed into the hands of fervent supporters of what was coming to be called 'the Revolution'. A succession of similar revolts, set off by news from Paris, effected a transfer of power in many provincial towns. The old centralised royal government collapsed; the King's orders were obeyed only if they were endorsed by the National Assembly (**25**, ch. 3; **100**, ch. 9; **106**; **116**).

Royalist and conservative historians later claimed that the *vainqueurs de la Bastille* (conquerors of the Bastille) were the 'floating population' – criminal rabble in the pay of freemasons, Orleanists and *philosophes*. In fact such people were not involved in disturbances. Dangerous as individuals, they lacked organisation, the habit of acting together, and strong common interests to push them into purposeful collective action (**96**). In fact five-sixths of the 700–800 whose addresses and occupations are known were artisans, masters or journeymen; for example joiners, locksmiths, cobblers, shopkeepers and clock-makers. Such workers were subject to intense pressure from the decline in purchasing power of wages and incomes. It was on 14 July itself that the price of a loaf reached 16 *sous*, the highest level since 1770. The remaining sixth of the *vainqueurs* included more prosperous traders, soldiers and members of the liberal professions enrolled in the National Guard.

The immediate consequences of 14 July were soon apparent. Royal plans for a counter-offensive against Paris and a Royal Session at Versailles to overawe the Assembly had to be abandoned. After meeting his advisers, Louis agreed to recall Necker and order the withdrawal of troops from Paris and Versailles. Three days after the fall of the Bastille he was persuaded to go to Paris, accompanied by a procession of deputies, to speak briefly from the steps of the Hôtel de Ville (City Hall) and put in his hat the new Revolutionary cockade of red, white and blue. Thomas Jefferson, then American Resident in Paris, commented: 'Such an *amende honorable* . . . no sovereign ever made and no people ever received'. Any hope of the King arresting the course of the Revolution was now gone. News of the fall of the Bastille was reported all over the world, usually in terms of the dawn of a new age of liberty. There was dancing in the streets of St Petersburg and Caracas, while in Königsberg (Kaliningrad) the great philosopher Immanuel Kant broke the habit of a lifetime and abandoned his afternoon walk to read about the taking of the Bastille.

In France itself there was widespread rejoicing. The first issue of the newspaper *Les Révolutions de Paris* ('Paris Revolutions') declared on 17 July: 'The events of that glorious day will astonish our enemies and foretell at last the triumph of justice and liberty'. With the end of 'royal absolutism' and the transfer of sovereign authority to the National Assembly, the Court party began to disintegrate and some eminent nobles, including the King's brothers, left for the frontier.

Censorship of the press vanished. In Paris there was a revolution in municipal government, power passing into the hands of the committee of property-owning electors who had organised the National Guard and now formed the new Paris Commune\*. Beneath the surface there was some tension, for the electors were concerned about the possible destruction of property and the threat of 'anarchy'; hence their reluctance to permit the indiscriminate distribution of arms. Neither had they welcomed the attacks on the *barrières* (customs posts) and prisons. Such tensions and anxieties were to reappear in the future, but in July 1789 they were largely swept aside by popular enthusiasm for liberty and fear of an aristocratic counter-offensive.

## The Downfall of the *Ancien Régime*

It is possible to view the events of July 1789 as the climax of a national revolution which had its origins in the aristocratic revolt of 1787 and began in earnest in January 1789. If the people of the capital had been stimulated by the example of provinces like Brittany and Dauphiné, which some of them had recently left, then the process was reversed after the fall of the Bastille. Provincial revolutions were now inspired by news of events in Paris. Some were failures, but others succeeded in removing established oligarchies, controlling the price of bread, and creating companies of the National Guard, designed, as in Paris, to curb both aristocratic reaction and popular disturbances (**115**). As *intendants* fled, so the breakdown of royal authority and the *de facto* decentralisation of French government were both confirmed. Euphoria at the news of the Bastille also prompted most people to cease paying taxes, which were widely regarded as being swept away with the *ancien régime*. This development was not congenial to the Assembly, which had inherited the royal deficit and was desperately hungry for revenue (**99**).

News of the fall of the Bastille also provided further incitement for peasant revolts, which had been taking place in parts of France since December 1788. The failure of the Assembly to tackle peasant grievances was put down to the 'aristocratic plot'. Seigneurial dues, while their incidence greatly varied in different parts of the country, weighed more heavily on the peasantry in the spring of 1789 when in many places bread prices were even higher than in Paris. The result was an increase in peasant attacks on walls and fences of enclosed fields, accompanied by reoccupation of former common lands and a suspension of payment of tithes and feudal dues (**258**, ch. 3). From 20 July to 16 August the 'Great Fear' was at its height in eight regions of France. Rumours of an aristocratic counter-revolution, when *émigrés* would return at the head of hordes of Pied-montese or Spanish brigands and foreign mercenaries, were fed by the dispersal of military units from Paris to the countryside and by the despatch of troops from the towns to requisition grain. Intense alarm spread over much of France. The brigands, it was alleged, would burn the ripening corn in the fields as the crucial initial stage in a plot to starve the people into submission (*pacte de famine*). When the brigands failed to materialise and no crops were destroyed, the peasants turned on the *châteaux*, many of which were razed to the ground once the manorial rolls, recording seigneurial obligations, had been destroyed. The *seigneurs* themselves were not always safe; in the Lodève some were shot from behind hedges. Yet large tracts of the French countryside were not affected by the peasant disturb-ances. In many places, as in the Périgord, near Bordeaux, cus-tomary festive celebrations continued as normal through the summer (**113**, chs 5–6; **62**, ch. 10; **153**, ch. 4) [**doc. 2**].

Although peasant violence had been endemic since the beginning of the year, the revolt of late July and early August took the National Assembly unawares. With its victory over the King and the Court consummated on 14 July, the Assembly wished to get on with its self-appointed task of preparing a Declaration of Rights and a Con-stitution. On 7 July it began calling itself the National Constituent Assembly. Most deputies had disapproved of the violence in Paris and the provincial municipalities, even though such violence had been partly inspired and guided by bourgeois leaders who normally displayed due respect for property. But the peasant revolt had been carried through by small proprietors and agricultural labourers who had not hesitated to attack property, whether it belonged to noble *seigneurs* or prosperous bourgeois. The Paris newspapers denounced peasant rebels as bandits who ought to be firmly repressed (**120**). Moreover, peasants opposed the economic liberalism of the deputies, preferring strict regulation of the grain trade and bread prices, as well as a restoration of traditional agricultural customary organisation in areas where it had been undermined, like the Paris cereal region. They had little enthusiasm for capitalist farming and new agrarian techniques.

These peasant attitudes had been at the core of many of the rural *cahiers*, which some members of the Assembly had helped water down before setting out for Versailles. Members of the Third Estate had never aimed at the complete destruction of seigneurial rights, especially since quite a number themselves owned such rights. Besides, if feudal dues and property were to be destroyed, then it should be by legal means, with due compensation, not by unbridled insurrection (**61**, ch. 11; **19**, ch. 3; **258**, ch. 4). At bottom, there was little sympathy for the peasant insurgents. In contrast to the fêted 'Conquerors of the Bastille', many peasants were tried and executed amid the silence of the Paris press. National Guards from the towns sallied forth to 'punish' insurrectionary villages.

Despite this latent hostility towards the peasant revolt, the Assembly was obliged to make concessions. Public order and private property could be maintained only by giving some sort of legal sanction to the peasants' actions, for the resources were lacking for the only alternative, full-scale repression, given the dispersal of military forces and a disintegrating royal army. In any case, the Assembly needed the support of the peasantry, who accounted for a majority of the population. On the night of 4 August 1789, wealthy members of the liberal aristocracy, headed by those of the Court nobility who felt resentful at snubs from the Queen, took the lead in denouncing their feudal privileges. Impassioned speeches built up into a crescendo of grandiloquent renunciation by votaries of Rousseau (**111**). Seigneurial justice, hunting rights, fiscal exemptions, tithes in kind, venal and judicial offices, provincial and municipal privileges – all were abandoned. As one moderate noble wrote: 'It was the moment of patriotic drunkenness'.

In the sober light of common day, it dawned on deputies that they had overnight abolished most of the central institutions of France. When emotions began to cool over the next few days, the conservative instincts of many property-holders and lawyers in the Assembly reasserted themselves. It turned out that the feudal regime was not, as had been announced and as peasants all over France assumed, 'entirely destroyed'. Contractual feudal dues were to be subject to redemption by individual purchase, a qualification which immediately angered and disillusioned the peasants. The burning of manorial rolls had not therefore erased feudal obligations, and peasants were to carry on paying, for the time being, even the hated tithes, whose monetary equivalent was frequently added to rents, and harvest dues. Yet widespread conflict and peasant rebellion against payment continued through to 1792 and culminated with the Convention cancelling the remaining debts in 1793 (**258**, ch. 3; **19**, ch. 3; **35**, ch. 5; **62**, ch. 12; **25**, ch. 3; **265**, ch. 5). It was not the National Assembly, but the peasants, who destroyed the feudal regime by refusing to co-operate in its orderly abolition over time.

The Declaration of the Rights of Man and the Citizen on 26 August 1789, intended as a preamble to the Constitution, was at the same time an attempt not only to outshine the English Bill of Rights and the American Declaration of Independence, but also to take the wind out of the sails of potential counter-revolution. Bourgeois individualism provided the essential spirit of the Declaration [**doc. 3**]. Natural rights and national sovereignty were the two essential doctrines. 'Liberty, property, security and resistance to oppression' were affirmed as natural rights, leading to equality before the law and in taxation. Freedom of speech, liberty of the press and (rather grudgingly) toleration of religious opinions, were also affirmed. All citizens were declared to have the right to share in making laws, either personally or through representatives.

The bourgeois spirit of the document very much came out in the emphasis on property as 'an inviolable and sacred right' and on the necessity for compensation if property (that is, seigneurial dues) was expropriated. Political and social equality were, significantly, not mentioned. Neither were rights of petition and assembly, education or poor relief. On the other hand, the suggestion of Sieyès that the document include a section on the duties of citizens was rejected. Despite these qualifications, the Declaration was to inspire thousands of aspiring European revolutionaries, and there remains some justification for Aulard's view that it was 'the death certificate of the *ancien régime*'.

The sovereignty of the people meant that France was no longer the personal property of the Most Christian King of France and Navarre. Equality before the law meant the end of privilege. The provision that no man could be arrested or detained except by lawful means put an end to arbitrary arrest. The presumption that an accused person was innocent until proved guilty removed the justification for torture. Resistance to oppression conferred retrospective legality on the insurrection of 14 July. The Declaration was as much a product of specific historical circumstances, including demands expressed in the *cahiers* of all three estates, as an abstract prescription for the New Jerusalem. It expressed satisfaction with the destruction of the irresponsible government of the *ancien régime*, and it was inspired by the self-confidence of the energetic leaders of the Assembly who felt that they were about to transform the world (**61**, ch. 12). At the same time, Norman Hampson has pointed out, it was a very Rousseauist document. Subjects were to become citizens. The individual could only fulfil himself in a polity whose values were defined communally. In practice the Assembly was to do the defining, for the last sentence of the preamble made it clear that the people had no right to want what the Assembly decided would be bad for them. If necessary, in Rousseau's notorious words, men were to be 'forced to be free' (**25**, ch. 4; **264**, part i).

However, the gains of the summer of 1789 were not consolidated until October. Louis XVI refused to accept either the decrees on feudal dues or the Declaration of Rights, thereby threatening to undermine the whole of the work of the National Assembly. And he still possessed the loyalty of the hard core of the counter-revolutionary Court party. There was also, in the Assembly, a group of revolutionary leaders – the *monarchiens* – who had already evolved towards a political and social conservatism which aimed at providing France with a constitutional monarchy in which the King would retain considerable executive power, as well as the right of vetoing legislation, and there would be an upper chamber composed of non-elected notables to restrain the enthusiasm of the National Assembly. Only substantial property owners should possess the electoral franchise. In the event, the suggestion for an upper chamber was rejected, but the question of the veto caused such prolonged debate and political manoeuvring that the progress of the Revolution seemed almost at a standstill (**25**, ch. 4; **102**). A breakthrough occurred in September when Louis XVI, under increasing pressure from the Assembly to endorse the August decrees, summoned the Flanders regiment to Versailles. They were welcomed at a drunken banquet, with guests wearing the white cockade of the Bourbons and the black of the Habsburgs, while trampling the *tricolore* underfoot in an orgy of royalist fervour. When news of this reached Paris, it acted as a goad to the common people who, encouraged by radical journalists and politicians, demanded that the King be removed from Versailles and the 'corrupt' influence of the Court.

Despite the relatively good harvest of 1789, the price of bread had risen again, drought having put many corn mills out of action [**doc. 4**]. On 5 October market women marched from Paris to Versailles, accompanied by the National Guard under Lafayette, former commander of the French army in the American War of Independence. Reaching the palace, they persuaded the King and royal family to leave for Paris, away from nefarious aristocratic influences. Before departing, Louis accepted the August decrees and the Declaration of Rights. Henceforth he was to be little more than a cipher and the logic of his situation, as well as the attitude of radical politicians in the Cordeliers Club*, pointed towards a republic. But nobody had the courage to demand one while there was still considerable overt support for a constitutional monarchy. The royal family was soon followed to Paris by the Assembly, which subsequently met in the *Manège*, an airless and smelly former indoor riding arena. The Assembly, as well as the royal family, had been humiliated, and was now much more directly subject to the influence of the people of Paris and metropolitan radical popular organisations. The public galleries in the new Assembly held several hundred people, capable of intimidating deputies who dared say anything they did not wish to hear. Ominously for the future, many clerical members were shouted down as soon as they began to speak (**265**, ch. 6).

The intervention of the people of Paris at a decisive moment, securing the consolidation of the gains made in the summer, transformed them into a major political force. Discredited by the 'march to Versailles', the *monarchien* group, headed by Mounier, president of the Assembly and hero of the 1788 'Pre-Revolution' in Grenoble, collapsed. Some of its members emigrated; others followed the example of Mounier himself, who returned to his own province to warn of 'Paris despotism' (**102**). All this had taken place because, as in July, the bourgeois members of the Assembly had been willing, under pressure, to operate in partnership with the Paris *menu peuple*. Yet any alliance between Assembly and common people was bound to be uneasy, for insurrection might well be turned against the educated and propertied classes. If the radical deputies were devotees of Rousseau, then they cynically distorted his doctrines by locating national sovereignty and the general will within the confines of the Assembly rather than among the people as a whole (**86**, chs 1–3). Hence the Assembly declared martial law, censored the 'extremist' press and imposed the death penalty for 'sedition'. The Revolution had not been sparked off by an aspiring commercial and capitalist bourgeoisie. It was now the professional and intellectual bourgeoisie who were in the driving seat. At this stage their chief aim was a period of political and social stability during which a constitution could be drawn up and new French institutions reconstructed on revolutionary and enlightened principles (**96**, ch. 5; **19**, ch. 4; **61**, ch. 15; **153**, ch. 4).

The Revolution was now irreversibly launched and the *ancien régime* beyond revival. Absolute monarchy had fallen and would be succeeded by a constitution based on equality before the law and the abolition of privilege. Although the King had avoided civil war by refusing to employ the troops at his disposal, the Revolution had nevertheless been baptised in violence, as well as radical oratory and pamphleteering. After all, the taking of the Bastille was an act of violent subversion. There were already many deputies, often leaders of the struggle against the monarchy in the provinces in the winter of 1788–89, who felt that the Revolution had gone far enough. All that remained, in their view, was to create and promulgate a constitution. Yet the obstinacy of Louis XVI, the intransigence of many leading nobles and, not least, the arrogant sense of self-importance among leading radicals in the Assembly, made a peaceful evolution impossible, desired as it was no doubt by many moderate deputies. The financial situation, where the deficit was combined with decreasing tax revenue, was already the worm in the bud.

## Reconstruction and Disintegration

Although the year 1790 was not so relatively calm as historians used to believe, the Assembly was able to get on with its task of constitution-making. France was to be a constitutional monarchy, but the power of the King and his ministers was to be severely restricted. While the monarch could appoint ministers, they were to be responsible to the legislature, not to him. A decision by the King to go to war had to be endorsed by the Assembly. The latter had full control of financial legislation, with the King possessing only a four-year 'suspensive veto' over other legislation. Chances of a royal *coup* were reduced by loosening the King's control over the army and strengthening the National Guard under the aegis of local authorities. Power was to rest largely in the hands of the Assembly, total legislative authority being augmented by much more executive strength than was enjoyed by the legislatures of either Britain or the United States. An elite of *notables*, a blend of noble and non-noble property owners, had taken control of France and was to retain it for a century. The bourgeoisie had become fully integrated into the political nation (**62**, ch. 13).

In spite of article 14 of the Declaration of Rights, the suffrage was restricted, the right to vote being confined to 'active citizens' – men over twenty-five with residential qualifications, paying taxes to an equivalent value of three days' unskilled labour. But the system of indirect election of the Third Estate in 1789 was retained. Primary voters elected secondary assemblies, members of which had to pay taxes equivalent to ten days' labour. Secondary assemblies chose the deputies, who were required to pay a silver mark (54 *livres*) in direct taxes. This was equivalent to fifty days' wages for an unskilled workman. At each level, as Sieyès argued, a certain amount of wealth guaranteed some measure of economic independence, education and leisure time, seen as essential for political participation.

Just how narrow the franchise was in practice is difficult to ascertain, for there were considerable regional variations, partly because of the differing value attached to three days' unskilled labour. It has been calculated that almost 70 per cent of adult males could vote in primary elections; 50 per cent in secondary elections; with a mere 1 per cent qualified to stand as deputy (**15**, vol. i, appendix 5). Even though almost a quarter of adult males were 'passive' citizens, the franchise was still the most liberal in Europe and more democratic than historians like Aulard and Mathiez believed. In some areas, for example the Sarthe, the distinction between active and passive citizens was never made and virtually all adult males were enfranchised (**258**, ch. 6). Given that the poll in Paris rarely exceeded 10 per cent, it seems unlikely that many 'passives' would have voted unless paid to do so. At both the national and the local level, it was the bourgeoisie who were the chief beneficiaries, as many nobles began to drop out of political life. In numerous provincial communities – for example Bordeaux, Marseille and the towns of the ferociously-divided Gard department – it was the bourgeoisie who asserted political control, with the formerly privileged orders being largely excluded from local government. Many of the peasants who were able to vote soon ceased to do so when they found elections too frequent, time-consuming and financially burdensome (**179**; **192**; **142**).

Constitution-making was paralleled by administrative, judicial, financial and ecclesiastical reform. Nobility and titles were abolished in 1790, as were the old venal offices, though not without compensation for the holders. A new three-tier uniform pattern of local-government areas was introduced, whereby departments, districts and communes replaced the jumbled medieval map of pre-1789 France, although the new administrative areas failed to make much impression on the inhabitants. In each area, local government was elected by active citizens. To a degree this marked a confirmation of the effective decentralisation of government by the municipal revolts of the summer of 1789, with France becoming a loose federation of departments and districts, with minimal control from the capital before the Terror. In Paris itself, the Commune, the new municipal administration, was to become the rival of the national legislature in 1792.

The complex, arbitrary and expensive judicial system of the *ancien régime* was swept away. In line with the Declaration of Rights, justice was to be free and equal before the law. New courts and tribunals were to be established at each level of local government, with a central court of appeal and – a rather sinister touch – a high court for treason cases. Judges and magistrates were to be elected from a panel of qualified lawyers; criminal cases were to be tried by jury. At a time when much of the latent savagery of the Revolutionary situation had not yet broken the surface, some of the humane ideals of the Enlightenment could be implemented. Torture, branding, hanging and breaking on the wheel were all abolished. Capital punishment, retained after long debate, was to be by decapitation, a 'privilege' hitherto reserved for the nobility (**127**; **25**, chs 4–5). In March 1791 the National Assembly abolished trade guilds and corporations as undesirable remnants of 'privilege'. Among the guilds were employers' associations, and their disappearance encouraged various groups of workers, especially blacksmiths and carpenters, to demand higher wages and threaten strike action. These workers' movements had the support of the popular societies in the capital and the National Assembly took alarm. On 14 June, on the motion of Le Chapelier, it prohibited all workers' organisations and concerted industrial action. This 'Le Chapelier Law' was to govern industrial relations in France until the 1860s. Le Chapelier himself was, significantly, a leading radical in 1789, a founder of the Jacobin Club\*, and prominent among the left in the Assembly. Yet by 1791 he was convinced that popular emotions threatened to undermine the work of the Assembly. The Revolution needed to be halted and consolidated; indeed his motion was partly designed to ensure public order and stifle local insurrections. Many deputies, also former radicals, were taking the same viewpoint (**25**, ch. 5; **265**, ch. 6).

The creation of financial solvency and stability was the most difficult problem facing the Assembly and one which it conspicuously failed to solve. Too many people, including a high proportion of the peasantry, imagined that taxation of any real weight had disappeared along with privilege and exemptions. New taxes on land, property and income made little impression on the deficit, especially when tax evasion was rife. Of the numerous schemes considered to avert impending national bankruptcy, the most important was the decision in November 1789 to appropriate and nationalise the estates of the Church and sell them off. In return, the state would assume the responsibilities of the Church for education, public health and poor relief, as well as paying clerical stipends, a principle already accepted with the abolition of tithes. Until the lands could be sold, *assignats*\* were issued. Originally interest-bearing government bonds, convertible into church lands when they came on the market, the *assignats* were soon transformed into inconvertible paper currency. While their introduction averted imminent bankruptcy, the result was a rate of inflation which produced economic disorder and promoted social unrest. The financial problem was therefore not so much solved as postponed (**126**).

There was more to the sale of church lands than pressing financial needs. Many deputies saw it as a strategic move against an aristocratic reaction. Not only would a salaried clergy be dependent on the Revolutionary regime, but the sale would create a new class of proprietors whose interests were bound up with the Revolution and who would therefore be prepared to defend it against counter-revolution, both inside France and from abroad. Moreover, there were many municipalities and families, including some noble ones, who cast envious eyes on lucrative church property. In the subsequent great 'national auction', prices were relatively low and payment could be made in instalments, especially advantageous in an inflationary situation. But comparatively little of the church land was sold in small lots. Most went to those possessing capital – in particular, the wealthier bourgeoisie and substantial peasant proprietors – although a good deal of the land eventually ended up in the hands of the peasantry after many of the bourgeois owners began selling out in the inflation of the later 1790s (**258**, ch. 5). The original sale was not intended to be an instrument of major social and economic levelling, although this eventually occurred to some degree when land was re-sold in smaller lots (**140**). Henceforth there were solid economic interests at the core of the Revolution. Whatever the nature of the regime, through to the Restoration of 1815, nobody seriously planned to restore the pre-1789 pattern of land ownership. In 1801 the Pope acknowledged that church lands had gone for ever when he accepted Napoleon's Concordat. As it was, the sale of church lands united the rising, active groups in French society against the crowned heads of Europe, while at the same time embittering relations between town and country in France, since anti-clericalism tended to be an urban rather than a rural phenomenon.

None of these reforms, however, went deeply against the grain of the remarkable spirit of national unity that had existed since the summer of 1789. The Church had suffered from a deep fissure between its privileged and unprivileged members; wealth and property were concentrated in the hands of noble prelates at the apex of the ecclesiastical hierarchy. The status, privileges and rights of self-taxation possessed by the Church conflicted with fundamental Revolutionary principles. Moreover, the bulk of the clerical *cahiers* had demanded reform of the most flagrant abuses, and the 500 clerical deputies in the National Assembly were prepared to assist the 900 lay deputies in what they hoped would be a purification and regeneration of the Church. There had been a decline in religious observance among some local elites; fewer were endowing masses and supporting Catholic fraternities, and less money was being given to the Church. At least, this was the pattern in Provence, and some other regions (**123**).

However, the bulk of the lay deputies, as opposed to a militant minority, were not the anti-clericals, unbelievers, Protestants and Jansenists (Catholic Puritans) of legend. Few Frenchmen were atheists, though the more educated tended to be influenced by the deist tradition of the Enlightenment, where God was seen as having created the world, rather like a clockmaker assembling a clock, before setting it going and leaving it ticking without further interference. In Catholic eyes such men, who denied the incarnation, atonement and resurrection, were infidels. They, in their turn, refused to accept the Roman Catholic Church's claim to be the only true religion, with a monopoly of the keys to salvation. Most deputies believed that some kind of religion was required to impose order and moral standards on those who lacked self-discipline and therefore needed to be threatened with the prospect of divine retribution. Many of the more intellectual politicians adhered to a 'natural' religion, centred on the service of man rather than the worship of God, and saw no virtue in clerical celibacy or a 'useless' life of prayer and contemplation. For them, a contemplative order like the Carthusians was little more than a parasite on the main body of society (**25**, ch. 9). As yet, however, there was no desire to destroy the Church or deny its mission to the people, although there seemed little future for some of the religious orders. On 4 August 1789 the Church lost its corporate status, right of self-taxation and independence from the state, although it was to remain the official Church of France.

Payment by the state made a great many pastoral clergy better off in material terms. Nevertheless, the clergy were the most vulnerable of all sections of French society and the seeds of conflict were already germinating. At bottom there was a dilemma: how could an established state religion, with acknowledged influence over hearts and minds, be compatible with the Revolutionary doctrines of liberty, equality and national sovereignty? Unfortunately the Assembly was in no mood for finesse. Not only was it under pressure from the vociferous and anti-clerical people of Paris, but the submissiveness of the clergy in 1789–90 promoted over-confidence and a belief that both Church and Pope would accept almost anything. The enormous gulf between pious peasants and educated townsmen was ignored. In the eyes of the Church, the Assembly's reforms thus far were a more or less legitimate exercise of temporal power. But to encroach on the spiritual authority of the Church was quite another matter. Such an intrusion came with the oath of loyalty to the Revolutionary government imposed on the clergy on 27 November 1790. This marked a crucial stage in the Revolution, bringing to an end the period of relative national unity and constituting the real origins of counter-revolution and civil war. Aristocrats and *émigrés* who resisted the Revolution were henceforth to enjoy a substantial measure of popular support. For many radical members of the Assembly, loyal to the doctrines of Rousseau, the claims of civil society were total. A unitary state could not tolerate the existence of any kind of dual allegiance to Church and state, for the elected Assembly should be the sole repository of the general will of the people and of their loyalty (**25**, ch. 4).

Religious schism resulted not so much from what was done, as from the way it was done. The conflict that was eventually to tear the country apart began as a controversy about means rather than ends. Everyone agreed that, tithes having been abolished and church lands sold, legislation was necessary to put the Church on a different footing. The Civil Constitution of the Clergy, passed by the National Assembly on 12 July 1790, was in many ways a sensible settlement. Cathedral chapters were abolished, dioceses reduced in number, parishes reorganised on a more logical pattern, the aristocratic monopoly of high church offices eliminated and reasonable salaries guaranteed to priests. Bishops and priests were henceforth to be elected by active citizens, Catholic or non-Catholic – a much more contentious proposal. In addition, some clerics stood to lose by the suppression of many parishes, while many of the non-pastoral clergy were clearly earmarked for redundancy. Even so, the clergy did not hasten to repudiate the Civil Constitution. They merely asked that the proposals be submitted to a synod of the whole Church. To the Assembly, with its assumption of national sovereignty, a council of the Church was an unacceptable rival, and decrees of the Assembly were not to be regarded as 'proposals'. The Church ought not to have the temerity to try to dictate to the state. Authority now became the point at issue. In the words of Canon

McManners, the leading British authority on the subject, 'the mood of the day was proud, suspicious, fearful, Gallican, erastian, anti-clerical' (**121**, ch. 5; **25**, ch. 9). It was in this atmosphere that the Assembly attempted to force the clergy to swear the oath of loyalty.

To its surprise and anger, only a third of the Assembly's clerical members and four bishops agreed to take the oath, despite the presence of a noisy anti-clerical crowd outside the meeting-hall. In the country as a whole, only seven bishops out of 160 accepted and three of them were recently-confessed unbelievers. The clergy split about half-and-half, with considerable regional and local variations. Deep animosities spread across the country. France was geographically split, for traditionally devout areas like the west, north and north-east rejected the 'constitutional' Church, while the centre, the Ile-de-France and the south-east largely accepted it. In Brittany, for example, the overwhelming majority of the clergy refused the oath, while the country people marched on the towns to attack local-government offices and their occupants who had done well out of the Revolution. Vannes was invaded by a peasant army of about 1,500 and saved only by the National Guard from the naval base at Lorient. Many sincere priests had to decide according to their conscience, or were put under pressure by theologians, patrons, their families, or the localities they served. It was often difficult to make a considered decision when 'constitutional' priests could be stoned and chased out of 'non-juring' areas; and when 'refractory' priests could be met with cries of *'le serment ou la lanterne'* ('Take the oath or be hanged from the nearest lamp bracket!'). Such a cruel dilemma could have been avoided by more patience and political skill from the Assembly. The bishops were willing to compromise, but the Assembly proved a victim of its own arrogance and insensitivity (**25**, ch. 9).

In some regions of high oath-taking, in Dauphiné for example, there was relatively little conflict (**122**). But in many areas peasants, encouraged by their priests, were turned against the Revolution, as opposed to specific legislation, for the first time (**203**). For most peasants, Catholic theology meant very little. Theirs was a social religion, with religious practice offering the opportunity to assert communal identity. The prospect of losing the parish priest was disturbing, but much more worrying were the proposals to abolish small parishes, which would have deprived many villages of their church and graveyard, thereby undermining the concept of a local community which comprised both the living and the dead (**258**, ch. 6). Those who defied the Assembly were drawn inexorably towards the campfires of counter-revolution. 'Patriot' became a term for those attending the 'constitutional' mass, and 'aristocrat' for those who did not (**139**, ch. 11). Municipalities were given extra-legal powers to bully non-jurors. The toleration granted by the Declaration of Rights turned out to be worthless. Indeed, the increasing hostility of the Revolutionaries towards the non-juring clergy began to rub off on some of the constitutional clergy and prepared the ground for the dechristianising campaign of late 1793. It was to be some years before Revolutionaries were prepared to accept the fact that, outside the ranks of many of the educated, France was still a Catholic country, and that what many Frenchmen wanted was certainly not endorsed by their womenfolk. Meanwhile the gaping breach over the Church augured badly for the operation of a constitution which demanded a considerable degree of national unity and goodwill on all sides (**46**, ch. 2; **124**).

The prospects did not appear favourable. Revolutionaries like Duport and Robespierre, who claimed that liberty and happiness rested on the fate of 'the first Assembly of the universe', were unlikely to tolerate contradiction, let alone opposition. The Assembly operated under the rules of majority voting, but the views of the minority were consistently ignored. Following Rousseau, those in the majority argued that the minority ought to accept that they had been in error and hasten to join the majority, who represented the general will. If they refused to do so, then they were enemies of the Revolution itself. Hence the radical left, who won the debates and disputes over the constitution and attempts to revise it, would allow no legitimate opposition or differences of view, particularly since they felt constantly threatened, or said they were, by 'aristocratic plots'. Nor were the people themselves permitted to express their opinions. Proposals for referenda on the constitution and major policy decisions were rejected. In the final analysis the elected saw nothing wrong with telling the electors what to think (**25**, ch. 6).

Yet many electors became less willing to be told. In several areas, large numbers of people found that the decrees of the Assembly had left them worse off and that the abolition of feudal dues (apart from arrears) and tithes sometimes failed to compensate for higher taxes and rents. Besides, some had profited from the institutions of the *ancien régime* and they now suffered loss of both income and status. In some parts of France such as Upper Brittany, the Limousin, the Nivernais and various areas of the Midi, the contours of counter-revolution were being drawn as early as 1790, when the religious issue coincided with economic grievances (**24**, ch. 3).

# Part Three: Jacobins and *Sans Culottes*

## 4 The Fall of the Monarchy

### 10 August 1792

On the morning of 10 August 1792 an insurrectionary force of about 20,000 attacked the Tuileries, although the King and his family had already fled the palace and taken refuge in the nearby Assembly. The besiegers consisted of Parisian *sans culottes*, National Guards who had deserted the royal cause, and *fédérés** from Marseilles, Brest, Rouen and other towns. Because the bulk of the National Guard from the prosperous western districts of the capital had become alienated from the constitutional monarchy and absented themselves from the struggle, only the 900 Swiss Guards and some gentleman-grenadiers resisted. They were quickly and savagely overcome. About 600 Swiss were hacked to death, while about 300 *sans culottes* and 90 *fédérés* were killed in the most bloody *journée* of the Revolution. Far from being the 'bandits' and 'brigands' of counter-revolutionary legend, most of those participating in the insurrection were petty traders and craftsmen from the Paris *faubourgs* [**doc. 7**].

The consequences of 10 August were momentous. Robespierre called it 'the most gorgeous revolution that has ever honoured humanity', while the historian Marcel Reinhard describes it as 'the bloody dawn of a second revolution, the creation of a Jacobin republic, of a war government, of what some hoped would be political democracy' (**152**, ch. 21). The King's authority fell with his palace and on the evening of 10 August he was suspended from office. In November, on the day after the victory at Valmy, France was proclaimed a republic. Meanwhile, Royal Guards were massacred or imprisoned, while the liberal nobles who had committed themselves to a constitutional monarchy found themselves marked men. As they began to flee abroad, the aristocratic Parisian high society which had survived 1789 began to disintegrate.

August 10 was also a major setback for the Legislative Assembly, which not only was obliged to suspend Louis XVI, but also had to accept the demands of Robespierre and the Jacobin clubs, as well as those of the *sans culottes*, for the election of a new Assembly, the Convention, by universal manhood suffrage. The new Assembly would be faced with a formidable rival in the form of the enlarged Paris Commune, which had replaced the old bourgeois municipal authority and taken control of the National Guard and the police, both now recruited on a broader basis, including the former 'passive citizens'. Because of its intimate connection with the *sans culottes* of the *sections**, the insurrectionary Commune was able to challenge the authority of the Assembly in the capital; furthermore, it began to send commissioners to the provinces and the army as part of its strategy of radicalising the Revolution. Several provincial massacres of refractory priests and imprisoned 'suspects' followed. The dethronement of the King and the final clearing away of aristocratic privilege led directly to a greater degree of political equality and direct democracy in Paris, based firmly on the victory of the *sans culottes*. 'Passive' citizens, who lacked the franchise under the constitution of 1791, were now admitted to the meetings of the 48 *sections*, which assumed responsibility for court and police duties and the hounding of counter-revolutionary 'suspects'. Successful pressure on the Assembly to abolish remaining feudal dues and to inaugurate the sale of *émigré* property was designed to obtain the support of the provincial population. In fact such support turned out to be rather patchy, given the widespread royalist risings in western France against mobilisation for the National Guard and the army and against the proscription of non-juring priests (**22**, book iii, ch. 3; **24**, ch. 4)

The origins of the 'second Revolution' of August 1792 can be traced back to the bungled flight of the King to Varennes on 21 June 1791. Since 1789 the powers of Louis XVI had been progressively eroded. He had forgotten neither the night of 5–6 October 1789 nor what had happened to Charles I in England. Although well-educated, he was also old-fashioned and conventional, with no experience of life outside the Court. However, he was certainly not the fool his timidity and irresolution in public made him appear. He had been unable to prevent the drift to extremist views inside the Assembly, or the escalation of violence outside. All his political actions had to be approved by the Assembly, which exercised full control over most matters of importance, as well as over the army. Louis eventually realised that being a constitutional monarch was unacceptable to him, especially since his role in the Constitution of 1791 made him little more than a figurehead, exercising much less power than George III of England. Besides, he and his family had been virtual prisoners in the Tuileries since 1789 and he was particularly upset when crowds prevented him attending a mass celebrated by a refractory priest (**3**, document 85). Ever since the summer of 1789 the authorities had been unable to suppress disorder in Paris.

The King increasingly saw the work of the Constituent Assembly as merely provisional and hoped that, with foreign assistance, he could impose a new regime based on the programme he had outlined to the Estates-General in 1789. Although he was strongly influenced by the anti-revolutionary views of the Queen and of his sister, Madame Elisabeth, he suffered deeper misgivings at having sanctioned the Civil Constitution and the clerical oath.

The early months of 1790 were a period of relative social calm, followed by peasant revolts against the Assembly's decree that feudal payments should continue for the time being. There were also clashes between government officials and local factions in provincial towns, especially those in the Midi (**132**). In Nîmes there was a major confrontation in June between the forces of revolution and counter-revolution, for the Revolution brought to the boil hostility between Catholics and Calvinist Protestants – the legacy of a bloody conflict which had lasted from the Reformation to the end of the Seven Years War in 1763. Protestants, deprived of civil rights before 1789 though they prospered in the textile industry, embraced the Revolution with enthusiasm and succeeded in excluding Catholics from representative bodies and official posts. The result was a massacre in which 300 Catholics were killed against twenty or so Protestants (**145**; **144**; **142**). The euphemistically-titled *bagarre de Nîmes* ('Nîmes brawl') was an ill omen. For the Civil Constitution of the Clergy undermined the basic consensus which still existed on many issues in early 1790; henceforth Catholicism began to move to the side of counter-revolution. Attacks on priests and churches in parts of the provinces, many of them 'spontaneous' and unofficial, laid open old scars caused by religious hatred, while inflicting new ones (**146**). Religion was not, however, the only cause of the social and political divisions which made more difficult the task of men like Mirabeau, Barnave, Duport and the Lameth brothers who were trying to make the experiment in constitutional monarchy work.

During the spring of 1791 new fraternal and popular societies in Paris joined with the Cordeliers Club and the radical press in bringing more humble social groups in the capital within the political orbit (**134**). Consequently, the fears of the deputies and the 'comfortable bourgeoisie' for their property rights increased. At the other political extreme were courtiers who urged the King to force a crisis and *émigrés* who plotted to restore the *ancien régime*; some of them were linked with counter-revolutionary groups in south-east France (**150**). From late 1790, under pressure from royalists, the King began more seriously to encourage foreign intervention as an instrument for amending the constitution. His flight and forcible return to Paris created an immense wave of anti-monarchical feeling and widespread fear that an invasion of France was imminent. All over Paris, royal inn signs and street names disappeared. Although the Assembly refused to depose Louis XVI – he was, they declared, the victim of evil counsel and had been 'kidnapped' – the fact that he had left behind a memorandum damning many acts of the Assembly which he had accepted at the time served only to compromise him further and cast permanent doubt on his sincerity. Both popular societies and left-wing newspapers, in the provinces as well as Paris, vociferously demanded the King's abdication and trial in what was to prove very much a dress rehearsal for the events of July and August 1792 (**152**, chs 1–4).

The flight to Varennes deepened political and social divisions, for the Assembly, full of moderates, and the municipality, in the hands of the prosperous bourgeoisie from the west end of Paris, rejected popular demands to arm the people and begin a purge of suspects and counter-revolutionaries. Popular frustration with the Assembly's unwillingness to declare a republic sought an outlet in the growing number of political clubs and acts of hostility towards priests (**131**). The prestige of the Legislative Assembly slumped with that of the King, for the popular movement had not forgotten the opinion of the moderate Adrien Duport on 17 May that 'The Revolution is over. It is necessary to stabilise it and preserve it by combating extremism. Equality must be restrained, liberty reduced and opinion controlled'. When Duport and his colleagues seceded from the Jacobin Club and established the Feuillant Club* of committed monarchists, based on a policy of co-operation with the discredited King, the conservative municipality took firm action against the popular movement (**129**, ch. 10; **25**, ch. 11). In the event, however, the Feuillants succeeded in winning over only a small proportion of provincial Jacobin Clubs.

On 17 July 1791 the National Guard, under Lafayette, attacked a peaceful crowd of 50,000 gathered on the Champ de Mars, a military parade-ground, to sign a petition demanding the dethronement of Louis XVI. About fifty were killed (**96**, ch. 6; **152**, ch. 6). Thus the divisions within the Third Estate were openly revealed. At the same time the small masters and wage-earners of the capital became, under the leadership of the Cordelier and Jacobin Clubs, an element in the Revolution which could no longer be ignored [**doc. 6**]. There was now a clear line of division between those who sought compromise and more or less agreed with the words of Duport on 17 May, and those who did not (**158**). Many who had been 'patriots' in 1789 now found themselves pushed to the side of the monarchy and the Feuillants by the burgeoning popular movement in Paris and by fears for their wealth and property. In the process they became heirs of the *monarchiens* whom they had despised nearly two years earlier. The alliance of differing social groups which had carried through the revolution of 1789 was now disintegrating.

The search for stability by Barnave and the moderate Feuillants, on the basis of a revived constitutional monarchy, was doomed. Neither the royalists of the extreme right, who committed collective hara-kiri by refusing to vote in the Assembly after 13 July, nor Robespierre, Pétion and the revolutionary democrats would offer assistance. Although the King, after an agony of indecision, publicly accepted the Constitution of 1791 (described as 'monstrous' by Marie Antoinette in a private letter), it had little appeal for the Parisian popular movement, resting as it did on a restricted franchise. Neither did it attract many noble deputies, who voted against it with their feet as they left for the frontier and joined the earlier *émigrés*. The greatest blow to the constitution was struck by the King himself when he vetoed the November decrees against the non-juring (refractory) clergy.

Increasingly the running in the Assembly was made by the Girondins, or Brissotins, a loosely-knit coalition of groups of deputies, the core of which came from the Gironde region (**154**; **157**). Not only did they seek ministerial office for themselves, but they also launched attacks on priests and *émigrés* as part of their strategy of pushing France into war against the wishes of the Feuillants. Brissot and the powerful Girondin press claimed that war would bring the Revolution to a climax, force the King finally to commit himself, unmask counter-revolution as well as intrigue among courtiers and ministers, bring economic prosperity – it was assumed that a war would be brief and successful – and unite Frenchmen in defence of the motherland (*la patrie*). The King and the royalists also favoured hostilities, though for different reasons. They hoped that war would put the Revolution into reverse and lead to the restoration of royalist and aristocratic authority. Robespierre's was very much a lone voice against war, depicting it as a royalist and counter-revolutionary trap. During a fierce debate at the Jacobin Club in December 1791, he emphasised the danger and uncertainty. If the French army were victorious, a dictatorship of generals might ensue, led by the ambitious and unscrupulous Lafayette. But if, as seemed more likely given the disintegration of the French army, the French forces were unsuccessful, then the Court would invite foreign armies to overthrow the Revolution. Brissot, however, constantly countered these arguments by claiming that war was necessary to consolidate the Revolution and bring liberty to the oppressed peoples of Europe (**265**, ch. 8).

It was the final campaign in the Legislative Assembly against the Feuillants which terrorised Louis XVI into appointing ministers eager for war. The enormous size of the *Manège*, where the Legislative Assembly held its sessions, made proceedings more like a political rally than a political debate. This allowed the Brissotin orators, especially Vergniaud, to whip up nationalism, Austrophobia, hatred of the *émigrés* and fear of counter-revolution. As Blanning writes: 'Above all, by creating the conviction that their political enemies were terminally decadent but they themselves were invincibly strong, they also created the illusion that victory was certain'. A growing bellicose popular atmosphere in the winter of 1791–92 deepened the expectation of hostilities. This feeling was a by-product of popular revolutionary fervour and fear of counter-revolution within France, assumed to be the only free country in an unregenerate Europe. Early in 1792 a young student wrote to his father: 'Our liberty can only be assured in so far as it has a mattress of corpses on its bed ... I am willing to become one of those corpses'. Such heroic delirium became more widespread and reached a climax in the 'conquer or die' patriotism of the *fédérés* during the spring. A preoccupation with blood, death and sacrifice was an essential ingredient in the popular revolutionary mentality and later in the social psychology of the Terror.

Pressure for war came from the French. Until the summer of 1792 the Revolution appeared to pose no threat to the European monarchies. On the contrary, the events in France of 1789–91 were generally welcomed as removing her from the ranks of the Great Powers and allowing other states to carry on unhindered with their own schemes of a further dismemberment of Poland. The *émigrés* had no more success with the Emperor Leopold of Austria than they had with his predecessor Joseph II, even though they brought the seductive Madame de Cassis from Paris to Vienna to exploit Leopold's fabled 'immoderate appetite for sex'. Frederick William II of Prussia was no more co-operative, although the *rapprochement* between

Austria and Prussia which dated from the Congress of Reichenbach in 1791 boded ill for France, who had no wish to fight Prussia but rather to restore the pre-1756 Franco-Prussian alliance. War came as much from mutual misunderstanding as enmity. The Austrians believed that they could intimidate the French into adopting more moderate policies at home and abroad; while the Revolutionaries, basing their view on misleading intelligence reports on Austrian public opinion, believed that the Habsburg Empire was tottering and would be swept away by internal rebellion once war commenced (**135**, chs 3–4). It was to be a war to defend a free people against aggressive monarchs. There would be no conquests or annexations and the French would never employ force against the liberties of any people. Only those guilty of plotting against France and her principles would be punished, while the lives and property of those with whom France had no quarrel would be secure from the impact of war. Every one of these pledges was to be broken in the course of a war that was to last, with a brief intermission, for twenty-three years (**136**, ch. 2; **265**, ch. 8).

The war which the French declared on 'the King of Hungary and Bohemia' on 20 April 1792 (Leopold II had died and Francis II had not yet been elected Emperor) 'revolutionised the Revolution'. The gulf which had appeared between moderates and extremists at the time of Varennes now widened, for there were more politicians ready to argue that extreme measures were necessary to survive assault by the crowned heads of Europe. Irrational fears and panics were intensified: for example, the belief that traitors lurked around every corner ready to deliver the Revolution into the ranks of its foreign enemies, and that they were linked to armies of brigands, counter-revolutionaries and Austrian spies who were allegedly concealed in the quarries and sewers beneath Paris, ready at a signal to emerge and take over the city (**152**, ch. 4). Such fears were lent some credence by counter-revolutionary outbreaks in Brittany and the Ardèche (**184**). Those who appeared in any way 'moderate' and anti-democratic were equated with traitors as 'enemies of the people'. These views were characteristic of the *sans culottes*, whom war pushed further into prominence. An army weakened by the unreliability of many officers and indiscipline in the ranks would have to rely on volunteers from the urban working population. In return the *sans culottes* would demand a voice in policy-making and attempt to push the Revolution in a yet more radical direction.

The *sans culottes* were also motivated by economic grievances. Grain prices rose rapidly in the winter of 1791–2 after a mediocre harvest. Civil war in the French West Indies created a serious sugar shortage, aggravated by speculators. In January and February 1792 there was indiscriminate pillaging of shops and warehouses for sugar and coffee, followed by *sans culotte* demands that free trade in grain, sacred to the liberal bourgeoisie, be abandoned and that prices be fixed by law. At the same time, rigorous measures should be taken against food hoarders, speculators, rich merchants and prosperous rural proprietors (*gros fermiers*). Peasants in a number of areas attacked *châteaux* before seizing and dividing up common land. High prices, insisted the *sans culottes*, were counter-revolutionary and deliberately engineered to sustain the *pacte de famine* [famine plot] and starve the common people into submission. This economic crisis produced further social rupture, with members of popular clubs and societies adopting the red cap of liberty (*bonnet rouge*) and castigating the comfortably-off bourgeoisie. Rich *messieurs*, as opposed to poor *citoyens*, were viewed in the same light as moderate politicians – the catspaws of counter-revolution (**152**, ch. 13; **96**, ch. 7).

War brought military defeat as well as inflation and economic hardship. The *sans culotte* and rabid journalists and agitators like Marat blamed treacherous generals, the King and his Court. Not long after the outbreak of war, the King and his ministers were being referred to sneeringly as 'the Austrian Committee', whilst commanders like Lafayette were accused of being more concerned to defeat the popular movement in Paris than the enemy armies on the frontiers. Neither accusation was wide of the mark. Anger against the monarchy, which had smouldered among Parisian democrats and the *menu peuple* since the flight to Varennes, blazed up again when the King dismissed the Girondin ministers and vetoed further laws against refractory priests. On 20 June an armed crowd gained entrance to the Tuileries, shouted 'Down with the veto!' and forced Louis to don the red cap of liberty (the symbol of the freed slave in the ancient world) and drink the health of the nation, to tumultuous cheers. Displaying considerable courage, Louis refused to withdraw his veto and the crowd was persuaded to leave quietly. There was no bloodshed and this revolutionary *journée* turned out a damp squib.

On 3 August the crisis deepened further when the Brunswick Manifesto appeared. This document purported to come from the commander of the Prussian army, but in fact was written by an *émigré* associate of Count Fersen (a devoted admirer of the Queen) and accurately represented the attitudes of the French royal family. If it were meant as a warning against impulsive action on the part of the Revolutionaries, it failed disastrously. The declaration that National Guards would be regarded as outside the laws of war and shot by the invading Prussians if caught bearing arms, and that Paris would be razed if harm befell the royal family, stung the people of the capital to intense fury. A wave of patriotism and renewed hostility towards the King swept along many moderates who had no desire to see their new-found wealth go back into the hands of the *émigrés* present in the allied armies' baggage train. The National Guard, which had recently democratised itself by recruiting 'passive' citizens, became seriously divided and the forces of order in Paris therefore weakened, as they had been in July 1789.

The Legislative Assembly, torn by a complex series of clashes and intrigues between Girondins, Jacobins, followers of Lafayette and the Feuillants, was paralysed as petitions came flooding in demanding the arming of the people and the overthrow of the monarchy. It was in this crisis that the *fédérés* and the *sans culottes* in the Paris *sections* continued to fraternise, before combining into the powerful force which attacked the Tuileries on 10 August and opened the way to the downfall of the Bourbon monarchy and the declaration of a republic. The Legislative Assembly was reduced to an impotent rump as power passed to the Paris Commune. The Jacobins, more deeply involved in the 10 August insurrection than they cared to admit, had triumphed. Ultra-royalists and constitutional monarchists were proscribed. Danton, newly installed as Minister of Justice, filled the prisons from 11 August onwards. The Republic was to be the instrument of the moral regeneration of the people (**187**).

## Sans Culottes

The great rising of 10 August 1792 brought the Parisian *sans culottes* to the forefront of the Revolution. Not only had they been instrumental in the overthrow of the monarchy, but the admittance of 'passive' citizens to the assemblies in the forty-eight *sections* of Paris also gave them a secure political base for their growing influence on the Revolution. This was to reach its peak between June and December 1793, when they shared with the Revolutionary government the administration of France and the operation of the Terror. Since the work of Soboul on the Paris *sans culottes* in 1968 and that of Cobb in the early 1960s on provincial *sans culottisme*, it is no longer possible to depict them as an urban proletariat valiantly resisting hard-faced capitalism (**159**; **160**; **161**; **163**).

Clearly, the *sans culottes* did not form an economic class, but were made up of socially disparate elements. Those who called themselves *sans culottes* ranged from wage-earners at the bottom to men at the top like Santerre, the wealthy brewer. Other *sans culottes* included Robespierre's landlord, Duplay, described as a 'cabinet-maker', but who was in fact a major furniture manufacturer also in receipt of 10–12,000 *livres* a year from rents. Lefranc, the 'car- 'carpenter', was in reality a prosperous building contractor employ- ing workmen. Revolutionary fervour caused many wealthy men to 'democratise' their occupations on paper (**108**). Moreover, many of the basic ideas of the *sans culottes* – popular sovereignty, the right of insurrection, the right of recall of deputies who displeased them, and referenda on legislation – were developed in 1790–91 by radical jour- nalists and leaders of the Cordeliers Club rather than by working men (**108**, 24, ch. 3; **134**).

Yet the bulk of the Parisian *sans culottes* were tradesmen, shop- keepers, craftsmen, small masters and journeymen, accurately reflecting the economic structure of industry in Paris, where large factories were rare and the average master employed between four and fourteen *garçons* ['lads']. Shopkeepers, wine merchants, petty clerks and former professional soldiers were especially prominent among the militants; these were former 'active' citizens, or even *notables*, and there were more of them in the *sans culotte* movement than Soboul allows (**168**). Even so, they remained a minority. Mem- bers of 'popular societies' were less than 5 per cent of the adult population of their surrounding areas, while actual attendance was confined to between 4 and 19 per cent of the members in Paris (**167**; **165**, ch. 2). The *sans culottes* did not include many from the very bottom of society; criminals, beggars, casual labourers and the un- employed and footloose (*gens sans aveu*) tended to be apathetic or even counter-revolutionary. The *pauvre bougre** of *sans culotte* mythol- ogy was not all that poor in normal times, although in the Years II and III of the Republic (September 1793–September 1795) he was pushed by dearth and high food prices to the brink of starvation (**163**, sec. iii, part 2).

Because the *sans culottes* included so many employers of labour, most of them admittedly on a small scale, they never developed a coherent economic policy clearly distinguished from that of the bour- geoisie. They did not oppose wealth and property as such; only large proprietors (*gros possédants*) and 'excessive' wealth. Combinations of wage-earners in pursuit of higher earnings tended to be regarded as sabotaging the war effort. On the other hand, small property and carefully-husbanded modest wealth were seen as virtuous, despite such phrases in petitions as 'selfish rich', 'idle rich' and 'useless rich' (**102**, ch. 1). Masters and men, living and working together, were too closely bound in language and culture for a clear distinction based on antagonistic interests to appear between capital and labour on any scale, though strikes and wage demands could be undertaken as a last resort. Social divisions were arranged vertically in the storeys of tenement buildings (the poorer the family the higher the floor), rather than horizontally. Like the peasantry, the *sans culottes* saw their economic ideal in the past rather than in any future socialist utopia. They aspired to a traditional society of small, independent producers, whom the state would assist by taxing the very rich and restricting the operation of *laissez-faire* and large-scale capitalism. This outlook was partly caused by fear on the part of many independent craftsmen and artisans that they might be sucked down into the ranks of a wage-earning and dependent proletariat, even though they also felt that manual labour had been devalued under the *ancien régime* (**201**, ch. 3) [**doc. 12**].

*Sans culotte* was something of a portmanteau expression. It denoted a moral and political category as much as, perhaps more than, an economic one. The *bon sans culotte* regarded himself as a superior moral being and the epitome of Republican virtue [**doc. 10**]. Such attitudes could, of course, be held to justify any degree of violence and barbarism. Manual labour itself was viewed as almost sacred, even by those who had never rolled up their sleeves. In his sparsely-furnished garret, the good *sans culotte* was a hard-working, honest, humble and rather priggishly puritan citizen; essentially urban and regarding rural dwellers with suspicion (the feeling was mutual). He was a good husband and family man, who saw women's place as in the home and who, if especially patriotic, named his children after heroes like Brutus or William Tell rather than the saints. When he ran out of heroes' names, he turned to those of flowers and trees, fruit and fish. Sometimes he changed his own name; according to Cobb 'the list of members of the *société populaire* of Perpignan reads like a seedsman's catalogue' (**167**). There was always a rather humourless, if not ridiculous, strain among the militants. The *sans culotte* looked askance at the 30,000 or so Paris prostitutes, classified as counter-revolutionary survivals from the *ancien régime*, even if most of them were former maids and servants who had been made pregnant by *sans culottes* in their teenage years. Bachelors were regarded as hedonistic evaders of family responsibilities. Cards, billiards, fancy dress and carnivals (other than government-inspired 'patriotic' ones) were opposed as frivolous distractions from honest toil and political duties. The only permissible outlets were swearing and drinking; *sans culotte* militants loved to hold forth in the *cabarets* [taverns] and much of the disorder characteristic of the sectional assemblies was a consequence of cheap wine on empty stomachs. According to the *Père Duchesne\**, their favourite newspaper, to drink water was a crime. These standards were, of course, very much the ideal; no doubt only the most militant and fanatical measured up to them.

The model *sans culotte*, depicted in popular prints, wore his hair long, smoked a pipe and dressed simply: cotton trousers, rather than the *culottes* (knee breeches and stockings) of the aristocracy and bourgeoisie, a short jacket and the *bonnet rouge*. Powdered wigs, scent, knee breeches, buckled shoes, flowered waistcoats, bows and lorgnettes were dismissed as foppish and frivolous trappings of privilege, with overtones of sexual deviancy (**200**; **201**; ch. 2).

Equally dismissed were the manners and deferent behaviour of the *ancien régime*. The good *sans culotte* took off his hat to nobody, used the familiar 'tu' rather than 'vous', and 'citoyén' rather than 'monsieur', where swearing in the colourful Parisian slang of the *Père Duchesne*. He tended to define enemies by their appearance: they were the 'egoists' who wore fancy clothes, spoke in 'posh' tones, looked haughty or failed to offer the fraternal kiss of liberty. Anybody who affected to despise honest working men was in trouble. A music dealer was arrested as a suspect for observing, at a sectional meeting, that 'It was disgusting to see a cobbler acting as president, particularly a cobbler who was badly dressed' (**159**, chs 1, 6). 'Aristocrat' and 'moderate' became interchangeable terms for those who in any way opposed the outlook and aspirations of the *sans culottes* or who appeared to look down on them or ridicule them. These pejorative terms were also applied to those who seemed indifferent, lacking the overt enthusiasm of the good revolutionary. 'Aristocrat' could include those who refused to buy *biens nationaux\**, the confiscated Church and *émigré* lands, especially the latter which were deliberately sold off in small lots; or those who failed to cultivate their land or sell it at a fair price; or failed to offer employment to labourers or journeymen. The term was also applied to those who refused to subscribe to 'patriotic loans', who dealt in gold rather than Republican *assignats*, or who speculated on the Bourse or in joint-stock companies [**doc. 11**].

As the Revolutionary crisis deepened in 1793, 'aristocrat' increasingly came to mean 'bourgeois property owner'. In May an orator in the Section du Mail, one of the most radical central electoral wards of Paris, declared: 'Aristocrats are the rich, wealthy merchants, monopolists, middlemen, bankers, trading clerks, quibbling lawyers and citizens who own anything'. Wealth always aroused *sans culotte* suspicion, unless offset by manifest political virtue. Hoarders and monopolists were regarded as hand-in-glove with large merchants, bankers and economic liberals in plots to starve the people and crush the Revolution – for *sans culottes* were ultra-sensitive to the problem of food supply and the price of bread, while they lived in constant fear of plots and betrayal to the enemy. Hunger, as well as democratic politics and puritanical moral views, was a cement holding the disparate *sans culotte* groups together. Pillage could therefore be justified as 'egalitarian' and 'revolutionary', in that it fed the people and struck at the machinations of hoarders and speculators, the visible vanguard or counter-revolution. *Sans culottes* always tended to advocate immediate and violent political solutions to economic problems and, with brutal simplicity, assumed that spilling blood would provide bread (**161**, ch. 3; **166**).

Despite the fact that a number of *sans culottes* were property owners, though usually only in a small way, there existed among them a deep-rooted egalitarianism. They believed in the 'right to live' (*droit à l'existence*) and in the 'equality of the benefits of society' (*l'égalite des jouissances*) both conspicuously absent from the 1789 Declaration of the Rights of Man (**159**, ch. 2). A family should have sufficient to live in modest comfort, especially enough bread of good quality flour. No rich man should have the power of life and death over his fellow men through his ability to monopolise food and other basic necessities [**doc. 11**]. Food prices and distribution should be controlled by law, while the government should take stern action against hoarders and speculators. Some of the more radical *sans culotte* committees, especially the Théâtre-Français *section* on the left bank – full of radical journalists and home of the Cordeliers Club and Danton's electoral machine – demanded taxation of the rich, limitation of rents, restriction of the activities of major financiers, and the provision of government-assisted workshops and allowances for widows, orphans and disabled soldiers.

Although the *sans culottes* affected to despise 'intellectuals' and the 'useless' privileged learning and arts of the *ancien régime*, they were very conscious of their own lack of education and semi-literacy, although they perhaps failed to realise what easy meat they were for. unscrupulous politicians like Danton and Desmoulins and rabid journalists like Marat and Hébert. Many of them ran schools to inculcate what they regarded as a 'useful' revolutionary education, more moral than intellectual, among the young Revolutionary generation. Children were taught to sing their *Marseillaise* and Revolutionary hymns, before parroting the Declaration of the Rights of Man. Some were even taken to public executions to further their civic education. Such expressions of fervour reflected the patriotic chauvinism of the *sans culottes*. They were fully committed to the war; indeed many obtained jobs in the war bureaucracy. Early universalism and a desire to spread the Revolution to oppressed peoples abroad soon evaporated when foreigners proved exasperatingly reluctant to turn on their rulers. When France herself came under threat of invasion, *sans culotte* hatred of the foreigner asserted itself. Cosmopolitanism of any kind became suspect. Even languages and dialects like Breton, Basque, Gascon and Provençal were condemned as unpatriotic. No attempts were made to forge links with foreign artisans and revolutionaries; making such links between French cities turned out to be difficult enough. Again, there was often a gap between ideal and reality. *Sans culottes* in a reputedly militant ward like the *Section des Droits de l'Homme* [The Rights of Man Ward] could be surprisingly timid and unwilling to commit themselves to positive action, as opposed to aggressive words and posturing (**168**).

At bottom '*sans culotte*' was a political expression, born of accident and emergency in 1792. Even a rich man could be a *sans culotte* if he had a good political record, above all if he had participated in the great Revolutionary *journées* like the Bastille, the Champ de Mars or the second attack on the Tuileries. The *sans culottes* regarded such *journées* as legitimate expressions of popular sovereignty, for they believed in 'direct democracy', a concept which had originated in Rousseau's *Social Contract* (1762) and filtered down to the *sections* through the Revolutionary press, broadsheets and speeches, Revolutionary songs and Jacobin Club pamphlets and propaganda. Authority could not be delegated, for the true basis of government was the people, sitting permanently in their evening sectional meetings to discuss laws and decrees of the government. Deputies should be delegates rather than representatives and be constantly and immediately answerable to the popular societies (*sociétés populaires*). The latter had the right to scrutinise the law of the Assembly, administer local justice and the police, and help run the war effort. Thus the *sans culottes* saw themselves and the nation as synonymous. A government defied 'the nation' at its peril, for the *sans culotte* insisted on the right to bear arms, especially 'the sacred pike', and to overthrow an illegitimate government by force. Secrecy of any kind in government was regarded as counter-revolutionary, for were not plots hatched in secret? All meetings of legislative and administrative bodies should be held in public; all decisions should be open and vocal; secret ballots were furtive and undignified.

Not only should politics be open (and therefore vulnerable to popular pressure); they should also be unanimous. The Republic was one and indivisible. Unity was necessary to defeat the internal and external enemies of the Revolution. Those who were not enthusiastically in favour of the popular Revolution must necessarily be against it. Dissent was intolerable, for the *sans culottes* cared nothing for individualism or the rights of minorities: 'the *sans culotte* did not think of himself as an isolated individual: he thought and acted *en masse*' (**159**, ch. 4). Constant vigilance was necessary to unmask counter-revolutionaries and those who dragged their feet. The informer and denouncer were not odious; rather they were performing their sincere patriotic duty in rooting out suspects and sending them to the guillotine: the 'people's axe', the 'national hatchet', the 'scythe of equality' [**doc. 14**].

Many *sans culottes* were simple, credulous men who saw issues in the extreme black and white terms of the uneducated. In periods of calm many were indifferent and failed to turn up at meetings, except when needing their *certificats de civisme*\* for jobs and allowances. Such calm periods, however, became rarer after late 1792, when the country was threatened with invasion, hunger and counter-revolution on a vast scale. At such a time, gnawed by hunger and excited by alarm bells and cannon fire, the *sans culottes* dramatised themselves in heady rhetoric, embraced and wept tears of joy over their heroes and friends, and brutally hacked their enemies to pieces with butchers' knives. Their excitability, bloodthirstiness, gullibility, conceit, desperation, suspicion of plots, of moderates, of rich men and priests, of peasants and the provinces, were to provide essential fuel for the engine of the great Terror of 1793–94.

## The First Terror

After the downfall of the monarchy on 10 August 1792, the *sans culottes* and the Paris Commune demanded immediate and decisive action against hoarders, speculators, priests and counter-revolutionaries, as the war crisis mounted daily. During the six weeks before the end of the Legislative Assembly, its legal authority came into conflict with the 'Revolutionary power' of the insurrectionary Commune. The 'conquerors' (*vainqueurs*) of the Tuileries sought to impose their will on a weakened Assembly which resented the Commune's threatening tone and was only too well aware that Paris was not the nation. Both Commune and Assembly took haphazard and conflicting decisions in the confused situation. When the Assembly sent twelve members to the armies at the frontier, with the power to dismiss generals and senior officers, the Commune sent commissioners to the departments to invoke support for purges of local government officials, the arrest of suspects and the creation of 'watch committees' (*comités de surveillance*\*) (**169**).

On 17 August, in order to rally the petty bourgeoisie and the urban masses, the Assembly gave way to some of the demands of the Commune and put the 'First Terror' into operation by creating an extraordinary criminal tribunal, whose judges were elected by the Paris *sections*, to try those suspected of 'counter-revolutionary crimes'. On 28 September a major step was taken in the establishment of the apparatus of Terror when domiciliary visits were authorised in order to search for suspects and arms. Municipalities were ordered to root out counter-revolutionaries, while officials and priests had to swear an oath of liberty and equality. Priests who rejected the oath were given fifteen days to flee the country, or be sent to Guiana – 'the dry guillotine'. Feudal dues were abolished where the landlord could not produce the original title; *émigré* lands were to be sold in small lots; births, marriages and deaths were subject to civil registration. However, the Assembly drew the line at harsh measures against hoarders and refused to make general the price-fixing adopted by some local authorities.

Meanwhile the military situation was deteriorating alarmingly. What had begun as a war of liberation was turning into a desperate struggle for survival as the Prussian army moved across the northeast frontier. On 26 August news arrived in Paris of the fall of the fortress of Langwy, as well as of an attempted insurrection in the Vendée. The enemy seemed everywhere. In an atmosphere of acute alarm, the Commune took the lead in organising the defence of the capital. Over 30,000 pikes were manufactured; arms were taken from suspects and given to the *sans culottes*; by 2 September there were about 2,800 suspects imprisoned in the capital. On 1 September news came that the enemy were besieging traitor-ridden Verdun, the last fortress blocking the road to Paris. 'To arms citizens, the enemy is at our gates!' proclaimed the Commune. The tocsin (alarm bell) sounded, barriers were erected and during the next three weeks over 2,000 volunteers left the capital to defend the Revolution.

In this tense atmosphere, fear of betrayal increased. A rumour spread that, as the volunteers departed, so imprisoned suspects would break out and hand over the city to the enemy. Marat warned the volunteers not to leave their wives and children before bringing 'the enemies of the people' to justice. On the afternoon of 2 September the First Terror manifested itself when a band of guards, *fédérés* and Bretons savagely put to death a group of refractory priests they were escorting to gaol. Prisons, monasteries and seminaries were then attacked by a crowd of shopkeepers, artisans, *fédérés* and National Guards in a series of repulsive and unrestrained massacres lasting until 7 September. According to the leading authority on the subject, about 1,300 prisoners were killed, 67 per cent of them in prison for non-political offences (**170**). The September Massacres shocked Europe, especially Revolutionary sympathisers in Britain, and repelled many educated and moderate Revolutionaries in France. Jacobin politicians who had been implicated frantically tried to cover their tracks. But the massacres were applauded by the *sans culottes*. With terrifyingly twisted logic, they saw the slaughter as a measure of 'public health', a perfectly 'legal' reprisal for the killing of *sans culottes* at the front through treachery and at the Tuileries by mercenaries (**165**, ch. 2; **18**, ch. 8). The authorities remained impotent during the crisis and could only turn a blind eye, while the *comité de surveillance* of the Commune, which Marat joined on 2 September, justified its collusion in the massacres as 'this step towards public safety, absolutely necessary to root out by means of Terror the legion of traitors hidden within our walls, ready for the moment when the people march off to face the enemy'. The Commune later compensated the murderers for loss of earnings while engaged on their grisly task.

The First Terror and the September Massacres showed the unattractive face of the new popular democratic Revolution, with its hatred of foreign invaders, aristocrats, priests and prostitutes. Its belief in direct democracy also provoked hatred of what it regarded as a weak bourgeois Assembly, based on a theory of representative government which seemed outmoded to the militants of the Paris *sections*. A clumsy attempt by the Assembly to curb the power of the Commune had to be abandoned in face of the imminent invasion crisis. Danton, Minister of Justice, seized his chance to goad the Assembly into action and become a popular hero by thundering defiance at the foreign armies in a series of powerful speeches calling on the people to display boldness and courage. Arms, horses, fodder and workshops were requisitioned. Women helped the men to barricade the ramparts of the capital and met in the churches to stitch clothing. A nervous bourgeoisie could do nothing to stem this tide of enthusiasm (**234**, ch. 5).

In fact the Prussians' advance was less formidable than it seemed, and on 20 September 1792 the French cannonade forced them to retreat at the Battle of Valmy. Victory was gained by the regular line army and the volunteers of 1791, while the Prussian retreat was accelerated by dysentery and torrential rain. Although the French generals had sufficient acumen to keep the untrained and ill-disciplined volunteers of 1792 well to the rear, the *sans culottes* insisted on claiming the victory and spread the potent myth that the Prussians had been beaten by an army of tailors and cobblers whose ignorance of military drill was far outweighed by their high moral and revolutionary fervour. That the Revolution had been saved was no myth. Verdun and Longwy were liberated in October; in the following month the Austrians were beaten at Jemappes and the French overran Belgium. France was free from a major threat of invasion until the spring of 1793. No wonder Goethe, an observer at Valmy, felt he had seen the dawn of a new era. Blood, terror and total war had marked the advent of democracy in European history (**188**, ch. 1)

Events between 10 August and Valmy revealed the breakdown of any political compromise solution. The pressures of war and fear of counter-revolution had undermined the Constitution of 1791. The question posed in 1789 – how was the state to be run once the *ancien régime* was destroyed? – was thrown open again. In August 1792 the rivalries between the Legislative Assembly, the Paris Commune, the Executive Council of Ministers and the general assemblies of the Paris *sections* had seemed to deprive central government of any purpose and direction, a confusion which had been only temporarily disguised by the exigencies of the invasion crisis in early September. Even the election of a National Convention by universal suffrage failed to remove the fundamental conflict which had developed since the outbreak of war between the popular and the parliamentary version of democracy, each claiming indivisible sovereignty, each linked to some degree to social antagonisms and the conflict between Paris and the provinces. And a basic problem had already appeared which was to lead to the French Revolution becoming a tragedy: how to reserve to the state the violence which had been unleashed?

## Girondins and Montagnards

The National Convention which assembled on 20 September 1792 was scarcely representative of the nation. Not only had various royalist and moderate groups been disfranchised, but a mere million had bothered to vote out of an electorate of five million. Its composition was much the same as its two predecessors: mainly the urban bourgeoisie with a preponderance of lawyers. Indeed sixty-nine former members of the Constituent and 190 of the Legislative Assemblies were elected. There were only two working men; labouring *sans culottes* found it difficult to get elected at either the national or the municipal level. For a brief period there was something of a truce between the warring factions of August; even the Paris Commune was willing to accept the overall sovereignty of the Convention for the moment. The monarchy was abolished by unanimous vote and the declaration of a Republic 'one and indivisible' was passed without dissent.

Such harmony was shortlived. Within a few weeks the Convention was torn apart by the dispute between Girondins and Montagnards, a struggle which lasted until the leading Girondins were expelled from the Convention on 2 June 1793. The Girondins were so called because a number of them came from the Gironde and Bordeaux area, while the *Montagnards* [men of the Mountain] derived their name from the fact that they sat high on the left of the chair in the tiered Assembly. Paris was the base of their electoral strength. The exact nature of the conflict has vexed historians. Were the Girondins and Montagnards tightly-organised parties? Was the conflict between them based on personal rivalries and the desire for place and power; or was it the political manifestation of a social and economic class struggle? While parties in the modern sense did not exist in the Convention – for in France, as in England, the term 'party' was pejorative, being associated with faction and disruption – it appears that the Montagnards were relatively well-organised, in that they were a small group whose tactics had often been concerted beforehand in the Jacobin Club, which passed under their control in November [**doc. 6**]. Certainly they were usually able to persuade the 'Plain' – the majority in the Convention – to support their policies against those of the Girondins. Modern research has made it no longer possible to view the Girondins as a coherent party, a view created by Montagnard propaganda and which persuaded historians like Lamartine, Michelet and Mathiez (**154; 156**). What loose ties there were between the associates of Brissot and Roland were based more on personal friendship and temperament than on any firm organization and common policy. The final victory of the Montagnards owed a good deal to their strong base in the Paris *sections* as also to the disunity of their opponents, a coalition of small groups more at home conversing in Paris *salons* than in planning concerted political strategy.

Marxist historians who, following Mathiez, have depicted the difference between Girondins and Montagnards as primarily economic and social, remain unconvincing. There seems little evidence that the Girondins were a party of wealth, representing the capitalist and high commercial and industrial bourgeoisie, while the Montagnards represented the lesser bourgeoisie and groups like artisans and shopkeepers. Girondin and Montagnard leaders were in fact similar in social background, while both factions were agreed on main lines of policy: hatred of privilege, anti-clericalism and economic liberalism. Apart from the Girondins' growing hostility towards 'the Paris mob', factional rivalries and personal quarrels were much more significant than ideological standpoints (**22**, book iii, ch. 5; **19**, ch. 7). At the time of the King's flight in June 1791 Parisian opinion had been polarised between constitutionalists and insurrectionists, with Girondins and Jacobins in both groups. Provincial Jacobin clubs subscribed to the Girondin, rather than the Jacobin press. The eventual division of the two groups into hostile camps only occurred after 10 August 1792 as a result of political tactics, when the Jacobins, dominant in the Paris Commune and the *sections*, were able to elect from their ranks Paris deputies for the Convention. Hence the Girondins were obliged for the first time to seek support from the provinces (**133**; **262**).

It may be true that many Montagnards were more concerned with social welfare than the majority of the deputies, but at bottom their economic ideas were also rooted in liberal doctrines of the free market. This is well illustrated by the issues of price control and grain circulation. The Convention abandoned the arrangements for requisitioning grain undertaken in August during the invasion crisis. During the autumn, however, there were disturbances in Lyon, where unemployed silk-weavers (*canuts*) forced the municipality to control the price of basic foodstuffs and tax the rich. These were followed by peasant revolts in the Beauce and the Ile-de-France, where grain requisitioning for the armies had reduced supplies and raised prices; markets were plundered as peasants demanded price controls. Such demands were echoed by the *sans culottes* of the Paris *sections*. Roland, the Minister of the Interior and a leading Girondin, argued that price-fixing would mean more violence, even civil war. However neither Robespierre nor Saint-Just, leading Jacobins, would accept price control either. Political considerations took precedence over economic distress.

When the Convention met, the Girondin groups had some advantages. They commanded considerable support in the Assembly, where most deputies were moderate men shocked at the September massacres and suspicious of the Montagnards, led by Robespierre and the twenty-four Jacobin deputies for Paris. Not only were the Jacobins known to have close links with the *sans culottes* and those accused of anarchy and terror, but the Girondins insisted on the maintenance of the law, the rights of the provinces and the sovereignty of the Convention. Besides, the Girondins held a virtual monopoly of ministerial posts. So the initiative seemed with them in the intense quarrel produced by the revolution of 10 August.

Partly because they were no more than a loose coalition of small groups, the Girondins frittered away some of their advantages. Their attacks on Paris as a centre of anarchy and disorder, their compensatory appeals to the provinces, their desire to be rid of the extraordinary Revolutionary tribunal established in August, their attempt to pin responsibility for the September massacres on the leading Jacobins and the Commune, their stigmatising of Robespierre, Danton and Marat as an ambitious triumvirate dictatorship: each of these alienated many of the moderate Paris *sections* which had themselves been shocked by the September massacres and could have been won over. As it was, the Girondins pushed the *sections* together behind the Montagnards, who consolidated their domination of Paris by gaining control of the Jacobin Club in November. Unsuccessful Girondin attempts to create a departmental National Guard responsible to the Convention, to counter the armed power of the Paris *sections*, brought a charge of 'federalism', though none of them actually supported the idea of a federal republic.

The Girondins certainly aimed at installing themselves in positions of authority. The Revolution, especially with the coming of war, had created a huge bureaucratic machine, with scope for exercising lucrative patronage in the struggle for jobs which could bring with them considerable wealth and power, as in modern politics ever since. At all events, many deputies of the majority 'Plain' came to feel that only the Montagnards, admittedly no less lacking in ambition, could supply the Revolution with a clear sense of direction.

By late November the Montagnards, assisted by the growing power of the Jacobin Club and its provincial network, as well as by pressure from the *sans culottes*, were more confident and made their influence felt beyond their relatively small numbers. The gulf between the two factions was irrevocably deepened by the trial and execution of the King. Demands for his trial had been made in petitions from Paris since before 10 August. The *menu peuple* of the capital saw 'Louis Capet' as guilty, by his treachery, of the death of many of their number. Proof that Louis was guilty of the charge of encouraging counter-revolution came with the discovery of the secret 'iron cupboard' in the Tuileries containing his correspondence. Yet there was considerable reluctance to send him to the guillotine. Not only would his martyrdom encourage royalist counter-revolution among those already alienated by the Revolution's policy towards churches and priests, but to destroy divine monarchy with a steel blade was certain to widen and intensify the war.

Debate on the fate of Louis XVI began on 13 November and lasted just two months. It was now that the terrifyingly abstract Saint-Just, deputy for the Aisne and at barely twenty-five the youngest member of the Convention, made his mark on the Revolution. To defend the King, he claimed, would be to condemn the Revolution of 10 August; the King did not even deserve a trial, for royalty itself was a crime – the King should die for being what he was, rather than for what he had done. Robespierre supported this cold terrorist 'logic' by arguing that to try Louis would be to put the Revolution itself in the dock and that the Republic could never achieve stability so long as he were alive. The Girondins were badly divided on the issue, as on most issues, some of them proposing that the fate of the King be subject to a popular referendum – a proposal which was to haunt them until their downfall the following summer, for in a referendum Louis might well have won majority support. But the Montagnards soon seized the initiative in what was essentially a struggle for the leadership of the Convention (**99**, appendix C). Robespierre, who argued that the people had already conducted a referendum on 10 August, managed to secure a system of verbal open voting by rote which, allied with intense pressure from Parisian democrats and mob orators, plus petitions from provincial Jacobins, secured a surprisingly narrow majority of 53 (**188; 178**).

On 21 January 1793 Louis XVI was beheaded in the Place de la Révolution, his final protest of innocence drowned by the noise of rolling drums. The death of the King may have pleased the *sans culottes*, but it threw down a gauntlet to Europe and, within France, created more enemies than supporters of the Revolution, as well as strengthening those who had already come out against it.

# 5 Anarchic Terror, 1793

## Crisis of the Revolution

Immediately after the execution of the King, the Republic faced a daunting crisis involving military defeat, widespread counter-revolutionary rebellion, economic troubles and *sans culotte* discontent. The crisis brought the conflict between the Girondins and Montagnards to a climax in two great *journées* on 31 May and 2 June which swept away Girondin influence and inaugurated what the bloodthirsty and unbalanced Marat termed 'the despotism of liberty': the attempt to save the Revolution by ruthless force and Terror.

The war had been extended and peace made remote by the opening of the Scheldt estuary in defiance of the 1648 Treaty of Westphalia, a move which posed an immediate threat to Britain's sea-going commerce. The edict of fraternity, promising assistance to peoples who rose against their rulers, the occupation of Belgium and the execution of Louis XVI also offended Britain and the other European powers. In February and March 1793 France went to war with Britain, Holland and Spain, thus taking on the three great European maritime powers, as well as Austria and Prussia, the two major landpowers. She now aimed at the newly-invented 'natural frontiers' of the Alps, Rhine and Pyrenees. Such expansionary plans were dealt a sharp blow in March when Dumouriez was beaten in Holland and Belgium flared into revolt against an army of occupation whose soldiers were regarded as oppressors rather than liberators. The outbreak of large-scale rebellion in the Vendée region in the same month put the Republic in deadly peril. Yet the central government was weak in a crisis of such magnitude. Political disunity and faction-fighting among politicians was more rife than ever, and strong central executive power still distrusted. Obstruction by the vigorous Montagnard minority made firm and efficient government impossible. As time went on, and the crisis deepened, it became obvious that new, powerful organs of government were necessary to deal with it.

Not only were there threats to the government from the frontiers and provinces, there was also mounting discontent in Paris, for high prices and unemployment had driven hordes of the hungry to the capital in search of work. Inflation, a consequence of the vast numbers of *assignats* issued to finance the war, pushed up prices. Early in 1793 the cost of a wide range of consumer goods increased rapidly. Soap, for example, essential for the work of thousands of laundry women, had reached 23–28 *sous* compared with 12 *sous* in 1790 (**172**). On 25 and 26 February grocers' and chandlers' shops were raided by market women who sold goods off at what they considered to be a fair price, although there was also a considerable amount of pillaging. A delegation of washerwomen demanded the death penalty for hoarders. This agitation owed little to the Montagnards, but was rather spontaneous action by women who found it difficult to feed their families (**176**; **24**, ch. 5). Robespierre rather sniffily criticised the *menu peuple* for being more concerned with 'vulgar groceries' than the power struggle in the Convention, but he never went short of his favourite oranges, let alone a meal. Marat, a rabid advocate of speedy 'revolutionary justice' against hoarders and speculators, became the *sans culotte* hero (**241**).

For a brief period the *enragés*\* [madmen, wild ones] came to prominence with a programme of controlled grain prices as a preliminary step towards a general *Maximum*\*, the establishment of the *assignat* as sole legal tender, a purge of the army and civil service and general repression of counter-revolution. The *enragés* never amounted to any kind of organised party, as there were only a handful of them, despite the exaggeration of their numbers by hostile government propaganda. Jacques Roux, the most prominent *enragé*, was one of the most attractive characters of the Revolution. A priest in one of the poorest Paris *sections*, with a following in the Cordeliers Club\*, he was genuinely appalled by the poverty and hardship suffered by the common people; hardship that was now so much greater than before 1789. Lacking all personal ambition and deficient in political skills, he wanted something done about the high cost of living (*la vie chère*) (**175**, ch. 10). In fact the *enragés* consisted only of three to five people, of whom Roux and Jean-François Varlet were the only two who really mattered. An extremist splinter group of *sans culotte* militants, they demanded economic justice, especially food for all, and condemned those who were making a comfortable living out of the Revolution. Roux, one of the few who was not in the Revolution for what he could get out of it, spoke for the very poorest of Parisians and could not be bought off or his dangerous doctrines silenced.

Robespierre and his Jacobin colleagues had little room for a person who was an unusually good priest and in close touch with the common people, wanting the Convention to do something about starvation, food shortages and inequalities of wealth. When the Convention failed to respond, Roux denounced it. For his pains he was to be hounded to suicide in gaol. Varlet, by contrast, was a young, rich, harmless eccentric and, posing no threat, was left alone by the authorities. In fact the *enragé* programme was no different from that of the delegation representing the extreme *sans culotte sections* which appeared before the Convention on 12 February and opposed the cherished freedoms of the grain trade: 'it is not enough to say that we are French Republicans; it remains necessary for the people to be happy; they must have bread; for when there is no bread, there is no more law, no more liberty, no more Republic'. Such demands widened the gulf between the Convention and the Paris *sections*, for the Assembly was firmly against control of grain prices, as indeed were most members of the Paris Commune. In any case, efficiently organising supplies was more likely to put grain in the markets than controlling prices. But *sans culottes* tended to blame the Girondins for resistance to price controls, although the Montagnards were no more favourably disposed towards them. On 9 March, the day that news of the Belgian revolt reached Paris, an insurrection led by Varlet achieved little except the destruction of the Girondin printing presses. Neither the Jacobins nor the Commune were as yet willing to take drastic action against the Convention, while only one or two *sections* came out in support of Varlet. On 18 March news was received of the defeat of Dumouriez at Neerwinden, followed by his desertion to the enemy after his troops refused to march on Paris and restore the monarchy and Constitution of 1791. By this time, the Vendéan revolt had spread through 600 villages and captured some of the towns in the region.

In such a desperate situation, the Convention was obliged to take drastic measures to reinforce the power of the central government: measures which amounted to the inauguration of the Terror. Eighty-two deputies were sent to the provinces as *représentants en mission*\* with wide powers of coercion to secure the implementation of the law of February for the recruitment of 300,000 men. Commissioners were also despatched to the armies to strengthen 'patriotism' by sacking incompetent generals and officers. A Revolutionary tribunal was set up in Paris to deal with counter-revolutionary offences. All rebels captured bearing arms faced the death penalty after summary trial. *Comités de surveillance* were established in all communes and the *sec-*

*tions* of large towns, initially to keep **an eye** on the actions of foreigners, but soon assuming police authority for counter-revolutionary offences. In such an atmosphere of crisis, the Girondins had little hope of realising their ambition to 'stabilise' the Revolution. Further measures soon followed. *Émigrés* returning to France with the allied armies or counter-revolutionary bands were threatened with the death penalty. On 6 April the Committee of Public Safety was created, to supervise all branches of the executive and to co-ordinate policy, although it proceeded cautiously at first. Girondins protested at all this 'dictatorship', but Marat replied: 'Liberty must be established by violence, and the moment has come for the temporary organisation of the despotism of liberty, to destroy the despotism of kings' (**241**, ch. 5).

The emergency measures of the spring of 1793 were not taken merely because of defeat beyond the frontier. In mid-March the great rebellion in the Vendée began, when, in Aulard's phrase, 'the Republic was stabbed in the back'. Armed rebellion on a massive scale covered four departments in a rectangle bordered by the cities of Nantes, Angers, Poitiers and La Rochelle. The explosion of the rebellion came at the end of four years of smouldering tension and antagonism (**183**). Sparked by resistance to the hated February conscription law, the revolt was largely the result of conflict within a backward area of France which had been undergoing rapid social and economic change in the closing years of the *ancien régime*. The heartland of the rising was the *bocage*: an area of hedge-enclosed fields, narrow sunken roads and dispersed villages and hamlets. Here subsistence agriculture predominated in a region where nobles possessed large holdings, where the seigneurial regime of pre-1789 France weighed less heavily and was less resented than in northern and eastern France, and where traditional religious loyalty was (and long remained) strong.

Conflict within the region itself stemmed partly from the fact that it was not completely rural. Economic change before 1789 had been spearheaded by a bourgeoisie which had established itself in towns in the area and challenged the nobility for ownership of the land. At the same time the bourgeois grip on the linen textile industry had been tightened; a new breed of merchants and clothiers controlled the livelihood of the domestic weavers in the *bocage*. On both counts they were widely regarded as interlopers and usurpers. Nobles, peasants, artisans and clergy resented the commercial middle class as aliens, committed to the Revolution and to undermining the foundations of a traditional hierarchical society. Hence the revolt took the form of attacking and devastating towns and *bourgs* in the region, places where enthusiasm for the Revolution and its meddlesome officials were likely to be found. At the time of the outbreak of the Revolution, the linen industry was suffering a depression which deepened after 1789, causing high unemployment among the artisan weavers, as well as further resentment of the commercial bourgeoisie.

To inhabitants of the western countryside, the Revolution appeared an urban, bourgeois affair which had brought little benefit to themselves, with conscription proving the last straw (**149**). To weavers and peasants it seemed to have removed tolerable feudal dues, only to replace them with higher Revolutionary taxation, as well as taking the administration of poor relief from the Church and giving it to parsimonious 'revolutionary committees' who tended to award relief according to ideological predilections. To nobles, the Revolution brought unwelcome growth in the power of the bourgeoisie in local government and cultural life; for the clergy the Revolution was a disaster, bringing the sale of church lands, which reduced their income, lands which tended to end up in bourgeois hands (**139**, chs 6–9; **148**). Peasant discontent had been growing before 1789, as conditions for tenant farmers and sharecroppers had deteriorated. Reforming legislation after 1789 drove deeper the wedge between well-off peasant proprietors and those with a precarious title to land. The tithe proved especially contentious, with owners of property profiting from its abolition, but tenants finding its cash equivalent added to their leases. Hence the rural community was divided, with prosperous peasant proprietors tending to remain loyal to the Revolution, but tenant farmers and sharecroppers joining the artisans and craftsmen in counter-revolution (**149**).

Revolutionary legislation on the Church in 1790 and 1791 brought antagonism to a head and led to numerous local disturbances and acts of violence. Nowhere were the 'constitutional' priests more harassed, stoned, beaten-up and generally resented than in the rural areas of the west. It was the religious issue which finally politicised the region between 'patriots' in the towns and valleys and 'aristocrats' in the villages and hamlets of the *bocage*. The February conscription law seemed an outrage. To ask for peasant and artisan volunteers to fight for a Republic which had increased the economic vulnerability of tenants and sharecroppers, had attacked the Church and executed the devout King, besides acting as the instrument of increased urban and bourgeois power, appeared deliberate provocation. The conscription order reached most local authorities in the area by 2 March 1793. On 11 March the tocsin rang in 600 villages, calling peasants and textile workers to take up arms in defence of the 'good priests' and Louis XVII, to resist the 'blood tax' of conscription, and to oppose those loyal to the Republic who had obtained lucrative jobs in the local administrative bureaucracy. The Republican government was unprepared for the rapid pace and scale of insurrection, as resistance to military recruitment was quickly transformed into a generalised opposition to the Revolution and all its works.

Between 60,000 and 120,000 men fought under the sign of the Cross on the Sacred Heart and the white cockade of the Bourbons [**doc. 8**]. Although refractory priests did not themselves take up arms, they were crucial in rallying support for the Vendéan 'armies' and organising supplies. Nobles were at the head of the larger armies (**139**, ch. 13). The revolt continued to spread between March and June, with the rebels capturing several strategically important towns, mainly because the Republican government attempted at first to put it down with untrained and undisciplined troops: 16,000 raw volunteers and amateurish detachments of the National Guard. Seasoned troops were required on the eastern frontier and to deal with revolts in Lyon and the Midi. On the face of it Republican forces had little to beat, for the counter-revolutionary 'armies' were scarcely armies at all. Unstable federations of local units, they were poorly-organised, weakly disciplined, and possessed only makeshift weapons and obsolete firearms. More of a home guard than an army, the rebels fought quick, intense engagements and then returned home. They lacked either the will or the organisation to occupy and administer the towns they captured. If they met hardened troops on a plain or defending a town, they were at a serious disadvantage. After midsummer, 30,000 regular Republican troops, many of them experienced veterans, were sent to the west and succeeded in confining the rebellion to four departments after the failure of the rebels to take Nantes, at the mouth of the Loire.

On 1 August 1793 the Convention passed a ruthless decree declaring total war against the Vendée. Republican armies in the west were reinforced with troops from Germany, as the government mounted a determined military effort and the rebels increasingly lost their sense of purpose. From mid-September the Republican armies gained the upper hand and the rebels were inexorably ground down before being driven from Le Mans and eventually annihilated at Savenay (Loire-Inférieure) on 23 December. Over 10,000 died on the retreat from Le Mans to Savenay, while another 7,000 or so died at Savenay itself. Fearsome repression followed. General Westermann informed the Committee of Public Safety that the Vendée no longer existed: 'It has died beneath our sabres, together with its women and children ... I have crushed the children under my horses' hooves, massacred the women – they, at least, will not give birth to any more brigands' (**258**, ch. 7). From January to May 1794 columns of troops combed the region, slaughtering villagers, burning farms and demolishing houses. Fifteen per cent of the local population of the Vendée area died; about 20 per cent of dwellings were destroyed. Some small towns lost 80 per cent of their buildings. Some historians have seen these barbarous reprisals as nothing less than an act of genocide.

The Republican government had to mount a substantial military campaign against the Vendée because the artisans and peasants of the *bocage* introduced a form of guerrilla warfare into western Europe. They used the thick hedges, sunken roads and clumps of trees to snipe at Republican forces before melting away into the friendly countryside. If the Republican government in Paris had initially not taken the Vendée sufficiently seriously, tending to dismiss it as a flash-in-the-pan royalist and/or English plot, they soon came to realise the potential danger. The long and bitter struggle in the west radicalised the course of the Revolution and provided the chief justification for the Terror. It was in western France that the Terror claimed the majority of its victims and where the worst atrocities took place. Deputies in Paris were soon to regard the Vendée as the major internal threat to the survival of the revolutionary regime. Not only did it pin down an army badly needed on the frontier, but the strips of Atlantic coast seized by the Vendéans were an open invitation for English and *émigré* armies to attempt an amphibious landing. The necessity of repressing the Vendée rebellion therefore lay behind the creation of the various institutions of the Terror at both national and local level. The Vendée rising, plus those in Brittany and Provence, forced more and more Frenchmen into making a straight choice: for or against the Revolution? (**175**, ch. 6; **258**, ch. 7)

Resistance to the Republican government was not confined to the Vendée. Rural revolts against conscription and in defence of the Church were widespread in the provinces, although armed risings outside the west took place on a significant scale only in Provence, where they were ill-organised, lacked genuine mass support and were more easily defeated. Whilst the alleged 'royalist plot' did not exist in the Vendée, it certainly did in Brittany, where troops and

National Guards were sent to check it (**184**). *Chouannerie* in the Rennes area originally developed as an anti-landlord movement, supported by tenants who had gained nothing from the political changes introduced into the countryside by the Revolution, against the proprietors who had gained a good deal. The nobility was expected to provide the moral and military leadership of the beleaguered communities, with the Church providing the spark to fire opposition. The Breton departments of the Morbihan and the Ille-et-Vilaine caused greatest concern, since columns of rustic insurgents threatened towns like Vannes. But in 1793 the Breton population failed to make a significant contribution to the war against the Republic, being relatively unco-ordinated and lacking any clear plan of counter-revolution. Moreover, Brittany was much better garrisoned with well-armed Republican troops than the areas south of the Loire. After early 1794, however, the Chouans were to prove a much tougher proposition (**141**; **143**; **258**, ch. 7).

There was also a series of urban uprisings in what the Montagnards termed 'the Federalist revolt' – the attempt to break free from the control of the government in Paris. In Lyon and Marseille, there were serious divisions among Republicans, so that the moderates and counter-revolutionaries who had been expelled from municipal government in August 1792 were now able to take advantage of the crisis situation and return to the attack. Lyon, Marseille, Toulouse, Caen and Bordeaux were in the hands of the 'Federalists' by the end of May. The revolt at Lyon, where the Jacobin mayor was captured and shot, was potentially lethal, for it gave the counter-revolution the chance to cut the Republic in two and hive off the eastern and frontier areas. In both Marseille and Caen, prosperous Girondin moderates gained considerable popular support for their seizure of power, since opposition to military conscription and the *représentants en mission* could, for many people, outweigh fear of invasion and dissatisfaction with high prices (**19**, ch. 7; **179**; **180**; **181**; **182**; **185**; **192**; **194**). At the same time there were sections of the common people who remained fired by Jacobin diatribes against '*les riches*', so that the Federalist revolts were partly motivated by bourgeois fears for their property.

Lyon, Marseille and Bordeaux, the second, third and fourth largest cities in France, were all developed merchant and manufacturing communities with a strong sense of local identity, fostered under the *ancien régime* by distinctive municipal liberties. In each city, more than elsewhere in France, the Revolution had meant the seizure of power by local merchant oligarchies wielding major political influence. Local institutions through which radicalism was promoted in Paris, especially the *sections*, were in the great provincial cities dominated by wealthy men. In all three cities the Federalist revolt was a mixture of assertive local particularism and defence of vested local interests, both jeopardised by Jacobin radicalism. Federalism was, above all, an anti-Parisian movement. There were, however, differences between the towns. Bordeaux, unlike Lyon and Marseille, had little indigenous Jacobin organisation and made only a half-hearted attempt at revolt, followed by very mild repression from Paris, with only 104 rebels going to the scaffold. At Lyon and Marseille, an elaborate military campaign and much bloodshed was required to put down the Federalists. In fact Federalism was doomed from the outset. Eschewing royalism and still committed to the Revolution, the Federalists continued to raise, equip and maintain volunteer regiments for the army. At the same time, they were clearly in revolt against the Revolutionary government in Paris and thereby undermining the capacity of the Republic to survive at a time of national military emergency. No moderate revolutionary movement could succeed against Jacobin ruthlessness and the struggle to win the war, a struggle which allowed no room for moderation and local pride. If the Republic were to survive, then it had to be one and indivisible.

## Fall of the Girondins

As civil war became a reality in the sumer of 1793, Royalist and Girondin moderates came together to defend order and property against a combination of *sans culottes* and Montagnards. Inside and outside the Convention the two groups became more closely associated with opposing social interests, as antagonism between rich and poor increased because of the economic crisis and *sans culotte* demands for forced loans on the rich to finance the war and subsidise controlled food prices. Pétion, the former radical mayor of Paris who had moved to the right, wrote in his *Lettre aux Parisiens*: 'Your property is threatened and you are shutting your eyes to the danger. It is war between the haves and the have-nots'.

While many Girondins insisted on regarding the Revolution as over and desired only to consolidate past gains, the Montagnards and their popular supporters urged strong government by a ruthless executive in the interests of social justice and, if necessary, at the expense of individual liberty.

By charging some of the Girondins with being accomplices of the treacherous Dumouriez, and others with being instigators of the 'Federalist Plot', the Montagnards aimed to seize power and impose their own revolutionary programme, although without becoming prisoners of the volatile and militant *sans culottes*. Through their newspapers and the network of clubs affiliated to the Jacobins, the Montagnards and Paris Commune publicised *sans culotte* and provincial Jacobin demands for the expulsion of the Girondin deputies from the Convention. On 20 April the Commune declared itself 'in a state of insurrection' until food supplies for Paris were guaranteed. A great popular demonstration demanding the control of food prices was held in the capital on 4 May 1793. The Convention responded by swallowing its liberal economic principles and decreeing the *Maximum* (fixed prices) for grain and flour. On 8 May Robespierre endorsed popular demands for the creation of an *armée révolutionnaire\**, a people's army of *sans culottes* to go out into the countryside and prise grain from the grasp of peasants and farmers who were alleged to be hoarding stocks in the hope of further price increases.

While the Girondin deputies were slandered as traitors and counter-revolutionaries from press and platform, the Convention decreed the arrest of agitators like Varlet and Hébert, leaders of an extreme faction who wanted a greater degree of economic equality. A commission of twelve was appointed to search out plans for an insurrection. But it succeeded only in provoking the insurrection it was trying to prevent, for *sans culottes* invaded the Convention on 27 May, got the commission dissolved and the prisoners released. During the following two days militants in the Paris *sections* assembled and 'fraternised', before establishing a 'central revolutionary committee' of lawyers and other propertied Jacobins anxious to keep the *enragés* and *sans culottes* at a distance. The tocsin rang on 31 May, while sectional leaders organised a revolutionary guard of 20,000 and put before the Convention a programme which included taxation of the rich to fund poor relief and subsidise food prices, a purge of nobles and 'moderates' in the army and civil administration, the creation of the *armée révolutionnaire* and the arrest of the commission of twelve, along with twenty-two Girondin deputies and two ministers. There then followed a brief lull, as the Montagnards debated whether to endorse so radical a programme, which would certainly not be welcomed in the provinces. Nor did they wish to see the *sans culottes* gain an absolute and bloody victory which would effectively hand them power; the *sans culotte* tail must not wag the Montagnard dog (**96**, ch. 8).

Nevertheless, the Montagnard leaders decided that they could break the Girondins in the Convention and at the same time hold the *sans culottes* in check. It was the latter who wanted the Girondins destroyed, for in practice the Girondins were no threat to the Montagnards, who could usually push through what legislation they desired. On 2 June 1793 a force of 20,000 from the *sections* surrounded the Convention and, without the bloodshed of most of the previous *journées*, procured the desired arrests. The *coup* marked the third great revolution, following 14 July 1789 and 10 August 1792. Stalemate at the centre was now over, though representative parliamentary democracy had been dealt a severe blow. An extreme but local minority of Montagnards had taken control of the Convention and the nation. Such a victory can be seen as an aggressive bid for power, or as a defensive action by the *sans culottes*, threatened by hunger, invasion and social reaction (**154**, ch. 7; **22**, book iv, ch. 2). There were elements of both.

The question now was whether the Jacobins could defeat the foreign enemy, put down counter-revolution and retain the support of the *sans culottes*. The latter assumed that a purge of the Convention would lead to the immediate implementation of their own social and economic demands. In fact the Jacobins had no intention of going very far down the road of social democracy (**186**). Nevertheless Thibaudeau, a relatively moderate Montagnard deputy, considered that 31 May 1793 marked the real beginning of the Terror and that now 'The National Convention was itself no more than a nominal parliament, a passive instrument of the Terror' (**3**, doc. 109).

## The Despotism of Liberty

The *sans culottes* got little immediate satisfaction: no *armée révolutionnaire*, no purges of the army and administration, no mass arrest of suspects, no distribution of arms among themselves. Montagnards were reluctant to be linked too closely to the militant *sans culottes*, as the Paris *sections* were still divided between extremists and moderates, while Jacques Roux's militant *enragé* programme met strong opposition from the provinces (**161**, i, ch. 1). Moreover, the Montagnards and the Committee of Public Safety were inclined to pursue a policy of moderation to justify the overthrow of the Girondins on 31 May and 2 June, *journées* which were condemned by the Assemblies of seventy-six departments. Federalist revolts stemmed not only from the desire of prosperous men in the provinces to maintain their political authority and social position, but also from resentment at the domination of the Revolution by Paris and direct action by popular militants against the legally-established Convention (**185**; **191**, ch. 2). The Montagnards' moderate policy therefore paid initial dividends. The Federalists were unable to focus discontent on the ruthless popular dictatorship, and although the Federalist movement posed a potential threat to the Republic, it did not develop to so great an extent as it might have done. Yet the fact that the Federalists were badly-led and lacked any central coherent political programme provided the Republic with only small comfort in a situation where at least a quarter of the country was in counter-revolutionary hands.

Unwilling to accept the extreme *sans culotte* recipe of violence, intimidation and strict economic controls, the Montagnards were nonetheless obliged to introduce some popular measures: the speeding up of the work of the Revolutionary tribunal, the resumption of the sale of *émigré* property, the division and distribution of common land in villages where the peasants demanded it, and the complete abolition of remaining feudal dues. But non-feudal contracts were to be honoured – in other words property rights in general were upheld. A further step in the search for national unity was the new Constitution of 1793, demanded by both Girondins and Jacobins. It included the principles of universal manhood suffrage, liberty of the press and the right of insurrection 'when the government violates the rights of the people', while the Republic accepted responsibility for providing a basic subsistence standard of living, public assistance for the infirm and unemployed, and universal primary education. But property rights were emphasised, the Convention choosing to ignore Robespierre's scheme for the limitation of property-holdings. Yet the Constitution of 1793 was very much a political manoeuvre and was never put into practice. Frequent elections would have meant prolonged political turmoil, with the Jacobins perhaps finding themselves a minority outside Paris; while constant referenda would have crippled the executive. Not surprisingly, therefore, the Constitution was literally suspended from the roof of the Convention hall under a ceremonial arch and deliberately ignored by the Jacobin leaders (**188**, ch. 2; **18**, ch. 9).

Although the Jacobins made certain that Jacques Roux was expelled from his *section* and the Cordeliers Club when he bitterly criticised their policy of conciliation, the Convention and the Committee of Public Safety were pushed inexorably away from moderation by the exigencies of war and rebellion (**173**; **174**). Early in June the Vendéan rebels destroyed a Republican army and almost captured the great port of Nantes. On the frontiers, July-August saw the Prussians capture Mainz; the Austrians invade north-east France; the Spaniards cross the Pyrenees and threaten Bayonne and Perpignan; and the Sardinians march across the south-east frontier; while in October came the invasion of Alsace. With the Republic on the brink of defeat, Danton made overtures for peace, but the fate in store for supporters of the Revolution was signalled by the action of the Allies in shooting and hanging all those in the occupied northern region who had played any active part in the tumultuous events of the previous four years. Not only was a massive military effort required on the frontiers, but substantial campaigns had also to be mounted against the Vendée, Lyon, Marseille and Toulon. Although Marseille was taken by Republican troops on 25 August, the royalists of Toulon handed the premier French naval base over to the English fleet two days later, while the bloody siege of Lyon lasted until early October. In Paris, the murder of Marat, the idol of the *sans culottes* and the Paris mob, on 13 July was rumoured to be the result of either a Girondin or Norman-royalist plot. France, it seemed to many, was riddled with treachery (**22**, book iv, ch. 2; **182**).

This compound of military defeat, counter-revolution and treason intensified popular pressure in Paris for ruthless action against external enemies, internal rebels, and those men responsible for local government in the provinces who seemed willing to resist Paris and its popular movement and reluctant to defend France against the foreign armies to the last drop of their blood. Only a new alliance between the Montagnard leaders and the militant *sans culottes* appeared likely to save France from anarchy and collapse. Only the *sans culottes* existed as a sufficiently powerful revolutionary force to sustain the government in crushing 'aristocrats, egoists and moderates' by means of organised intimidation on a grand scale. This line of reasoning among Jacobins in the Convention and government was encouraged by a hardening of opinion among the militant *sans culottes* themselves (**214**). After a prolonged struggle for power in the Paris *sections*, the moderates were swept aside and increased support was gained in the clubs and popular societies for a programme which included widespread arrests of suspects, speedier justice, the trial of the Queen and of the Girondin deputies placed under house arrest, mass conscription of the young male population for the army and the creation of an *armée révolutionnaire* (**161**, i, ch. 1) [**doc. 14**].

Apart from the desire for repression, there was also a renewed demand for strict economic regulation. The decree of 26 July threatening food hoarders with death had done little to surmount the spiralling subsistence crisis, the high price of bread and the downward slide of the *assignat* (**96**, ch. 8). Such a situation could easily result in another popular *journée*, so the government took swift action to head it off. Commissioners were oppointed to deal with the question of food supply, while *représentants en mission* were encouraged to requisition grain for the Paris markets (**162**). A forced loan on the rich was to act as an indirect food subsidy. However, none of these measures proved very effective. Much more dramatic and important was the decreeing of the *levée en masse* on 23 August, a measure which also had been demanded by the *menu peuple* [**doc. 9**]. All French men and women between the ages of eighteen and sixty were liable to be called up for war work. Widowers without children and bachelors between eighteen and twenty-five formed the 'first requisition' for the army, which provoked a rush to the altar by young couples all over the country. Nevertheless, by September 1794 the French army of 1,690,000 men, of whom 750,000 were fully equipped and trained for battle, constituted the largest force hitherto created in Europe. Recruitment on such a scale implied not only a new conception of 'total war', but also a degree of firm government control over key sectors of industry and the economy. Ironically, conscription helped deepen the famine crisis by depriving the countryside of healthy manpower and creating a chronic shortage of agricultural labour, except in mountainous or heavily-wooded areas where conscription was impossible to enforce (**163**, ch. 3).

As stocks of food in the capital continued to fall, so popular demands for general price controls increased. Women, always keen advocates of price-fixing, were bitter at having to queue for up to seven hours for unpalatable bread (**176**). On 4 and 5 September there were *sans culotte* demonstrations in Paris, urged on by the Paris Commune, for higher wages and more regular bread supplies. After temporarily pacifying the crowd with slogans like 'Death to aristocrats and hoarders!', the Convention was forced to make concessions. Needy *sans culottes* were to be paid for attending revolutionary committees and sectional assemblies, although the latter were now restricted to two meetings a week (**159**, ch. 5). A Parisian *armée révolutionnaire* was created, mainly composed of *sans culottes*, for use as a means of securing food supplies for the capital and of assisting the volunteer forces and regular army against Lyon and the Vendée (**161**, i, ch. 1). Yet the problem of food shortages and high prices remained. The Convention was obliged to bow to popular pressure and on 11 September decreed a new *Maximum** for grain and flour and, on 29 September, a General Maximum which fixed price for soap, salt and tobacco. It also stipulated that the localities should fix the price of other basic consumer goods at a level one-third above 1790 prices. To the surprise of the *sans culottes*, wages were also fixed, at 50 per cent above the level of 1790. Although in practice this wage freeze could not be widely enforced, it created bitter resentment (**97**, ch. 7; **188**, ch. 2; **19**, ch. 8; **223**; **96**, ch. 8).

Such measures cemented the alliance between the Jacobins and the Parisian popular movement and provided an essential foundation for the Revolutionary government which emerged during the autumn of 1793. The myth of consensus was now finally abandoned. Terror was 'the order of the day'. A new law of *suspects** on 17 September cast the net wide enough to include 'Those who by their conduct or associations, by their words or writing, are monstrous partisans of tyranny and federalism and are enemies of liberty' [**doc. 13**]. 'Watch committees' (*comités de surveillance*) were authorised to detain such suspects indefinitely. Terror in the provinces was paralleled in Paris by the trial and guillotining of Marie Antoinette, Madame Roland, the wife of a Girondin leader who had run an influential political *salon* in the capital, and the imprisoned Girondin deputies. Meanwhile a massive propaganda campaign was launched by the Jacobins throughout the country to rally support for the Revolutionary government against its enemies (**130**, ch. 7). The determination of the government was displayed by the ferocious intensity of the Republican attack on the rebels at Lyon, which fell on 9 October. Declaring that 'Lyon no longer exists', the Committee of Public Safety ordered the destruction of the houses of the rich in the city, henceforth named 'Villeaffranchie' (Free-town), and commenced barbarous reprisals which led to the lining up and blasting with cannon fire of nearly 2,000 Lyonnais (**162**; **187**) [**doc. 161**].

The Vendéans in the west were defeated soon afterwards, although violence in the Midi, especially when fuelled by Catholic–Protestant hatred, as at Nîmes or Uzès, could not be so easily eradicated (**144**; **147**). On 10 October the constitution was formally suspended and the government declared itself 'revolutionary until the peace', while the Committee of Public Safety consolidated its position as the head of the executive (**215**). Those who had done nothing for the Revolution were to be regarded as against it [**doc. 18**]. As Saint-Just put it: 'The indifferent must be punished as well as traitors; you must punish the passive ones in the Republic . . . we must govern with iron those who cannot be ruled by justice'.

# 6 Robespierre and the Reign of Virtue

## The Organisation of Terror

The consolidation of the Revolutionary government on 10 October led to a new spirit of vigorous administration. What was in effect a dictatorial regime, composed of a minority of Jacobins and *sans culottes*, imposed its will on the mass of the population in the name of 'the supreme law of public safety'. In a crisis of war and rebellion, the principle of decentralised government, accepted in 1789, was now reversed. New institutions were created alongside the departmental, district and municipal authorities, with the aim of subordinating the provinces to centralised rule from Paris, rule which was transmitted by means of *représentants en mission* and various *commissaires*.

At the head of the Revolutionary government stood the Convention, the symbol of national unity, but in practice increasingly unrepresentative of the nation as a whole. Although the Convention got through a great deal of work, handling masses of petitions and addresses and scrutinising the reports of government committees, considerable executive authority rested in the hands of the Committee of Public Safety (C.P.S.), the twelve members of which governed France in the Year II of the Republic (September 1793–September 1794), having come together on the committee between July and September 1793. Each of them originated in the petty bourgeoisie of the *ancien régime*, but they were of divergent social outlook and political opinions. If Billaud-Varenne and the ex-actor Collot d'Herbois inclined to radical, *sans culotte* views, then Lindet and Carnot were social conservatives. All four, however, as well as the other members of the Committee, were willing to sink such differences in the service of *la patrie*. The C.P.S. certainly worked hard: at the Committee rooms in the Tuileries from 7 am to noon, in the Convention during the afternoon, meeting again at 8 pm and working until the small hours before going to their camp beds. In fact all twelve never got round the green table at the same time, for there was a degree of specialisation in the Committee and some members were usually away on missions to the provinces. Only Robespierre and Barère never left Paris. Decisions were taken in common and required at least three signatures; there was no chairman and discussions were secret. Until Thermidor* (July 1794) the C.P.S. was unanimous in its collective opinion so far as the public was aware. It was a Committee of the Convention, which confirmed its powers for a month at time (**190**; **189**, ch. 2; **237**, ch. 8).

Something of a war cabinet, whose basic authority stemmed from its having been given oversight of the *levée en masse*, the C.P.S. controlled other committees, ministers and commissions, while delegating its powers to the *représentants en mission**. These constituted the most important single element in the structure of the provincial Terror and accounted for over a third of the members of the Convention during the winter of 1793–94, being attached to the departments and the army. Their orders were regarded as decrees of the Convention, for each *représentant*, wearing the *tricolore* sash, was held to be an incarnation of national sovereignty. A minority of them, for example Carrier at Nantes and Fouché at Lyon, were powerful proconsuls who ruthlessly shaped policy in their areas and had considerable freedom of manoeuvre, although they were supposed to report to the C.P.S. every ten days. The *représentants* were the chief agents in linking the departments to the Convention and the C.P.S. and in trying to force local authorities to implement the decisions of the central government. A France brought to the verge of disintegration by the Federalist revolt was to be coerced into acceptance of administrative uniformity so that resources could be co-ordinated for the war effort. To resist a *représentant* was to resist the sovereign will of the people.

In practice, the system of *représentants* did not work as intended, at least not before early 1794, and their activities contributed to the fact that the Terror was initially anarchic and lacked firm direction from Paris. They were sometimes in rivalry with each other; the same department could often be allotted to more than one of them; they frequently followed their own differing temperaments and opinions when establishing local terrorist institutions and repressing federalism and royalism. Javogues, the *représentant* in the department of the Loire, not only failed to report regularly to the C.P.S., but he also consistently ignored instructions from Paris, keeping in being the departmental *armée révolutionnaire** after the Convention had abolished it and carrying through an intense programme of dechristianisation in defiance of the wishes of the central government who recognised now that it fostered opposition to the Revolution. Insubordinate ultra-revolutionary *représentants* like Javogues made the Terror anarchic; by pursuing individualist policies, they prevented their departments from participating in a co-ordinated national system and weakened the concept of a centralised Terror (**191**, chs 3, 10, 12). Moreover, geography and slow communications between the C.P.S. and the *représentants* put a brake on the development of a smooth, uniform system. Messages from Paris took eight to twelve days to reach Marseille and a fortnight to reach the Ariège.

Besides the *représentants*, there were *commissaires* acting as agents of various bodies – the C.P.S., the Committee of General Security, the *représentants* themselves, the food commission – while also heading various repressive missions to the provinces, often in an attempt to enforce conscription. Below them was a further layer of *sous-commissaires*. Although these commissioners sometimes added to confusion, they were an essential element of the administrative and repressive aspects of the Terror, forming a direct link between local populations and higher authorities. Possessing considerable power at the local level, they were, like the *armées révolutionnaires*, instrumental in taking the Terror to the villages (**197**). The Committee of General Security (C.G.S.) formed another major branch of the Terror. Composed of twelve men like the C.P.S., it was in practice a ministry of Revolution police, preparing dossiers and inquiries, interviewing witnesses and despatching agents throughout France to undertake counter-espionage and root out those guilty of lack of revolutionary commitment (*incivisme*). It was also a committee of the Convention, but was subordinate to the C.P.S., with which it developed a certain rivalry (**220**).

Apart from the *représentants*, the primary instruments of Terror in the departments until the end of 1793, and in the Paris region until March 1794, were the *armées révolutionnaires* (**161**). Their task was to be agents of the civil power; to maintain links between the civil authorities and the armed forces; to ensure the provisioning of towns by prising food from the hands of the peasants; and to spread the Revolutionary message in an unenthusiastic countryside [**doc. 16**]. As apostles of Revolutionary orthodoxy, the well-paid and strikingly-uniformed *armées* aimed to instil fear in both counter-revolutionaries and the merely indifferent and to act as an instrument of vigilance and vengeance, working with local popular societies, watch committees and revolutionary committees. It was the *armées* which took a leading role in organising patriotic *fêtes*, in imposing the new Revolutionary calendar introduced on 5 October 1793, in founding 'schools of liberty' for the uneducated, and in attacking religion in the name of the trinity of Revolution, Republic and Democracy (**202**, ch. 4). Above all, they were involved in assisting regular troops in assaults on the major counter-revolutionary centres, besides enforcing the *Maximum* and trying to ensure the supply of grain and other basic commodities to urban markets. A practical manifestation of *sans culotte* attitudes and priorities, the *armées révolutionnaires* were concerned to defend the interests of the small consumer against the richer classes, and the economic interests of the towns against those of the countryside. Hoarders were regarded as the worst sort of counter-revolutionary (**161**, i, introd., ch. 1).

The *armées révolutionnaires* must not be confused with the regular troops or volunteers for the line army. Although they were under the authority of the military commanders in the war zones and under the nominal control of the districts and municipalities in other areas, they possessed a good deal of independence. Composed of citizens whose Revolutionary orthodoxy was guaranteed by their *certificats de civisme* and who were not subject to military discipline, the *armées* regarded themselves as citizens rather than soldiers. Officers were elected by the ranks and discipline was difficult to enforce, especially when a detachment could amount to no more than half-a-dozen dirty, swearing, shouting, vicious *sans culottes*. The origins of the members of the *armées* were diverse. The headquarters of the 6,000-strong Parisian *armée* contained some bright young men on the make whose Revolutionary credentials were suspect; many of the officers had been NCOs in the regular army or gendarmes or members of the National Guard. Those in the ranks were largely composed of the shopkeepers and artisans of Parisian *sans culottisme*, with their hatred of luxury, idleness, hoarders and religion, and their fondness for food and wine, together with intense pleasure in iconoclasm and destruction. Motives for joining were similarly varied: sheer patriotism, high pay, the need to flee creditors or pregnant girls. The departmental *armées*, amounting to about 40,000 men operating in sixty-six departments, had similar tasks to that of Paris. There were also some small 'unofficial' *armées* which emerged during periods of administrative confusion and anarchy. Some of them were little more than groups of bandits and gangsters (**161**, i, chs 3, 4).

If the forty-five or so *armées révolutionnaires* were a product of administrative anarchy, then they themselves did much to deepen it. Their areas of operation frequently overlapped and conflicted and there was little really firm control over their activities, although they were denied the portable guillotines they demanded. Sometimes they were guided by the *représentant en mission*, sometimes by civil commissioners, local popular societies and revolutionary committees. A few of them, for example in the Loire, remained firmly under the control of the old districts and municipalities (**191**, ch. 6). Just how effective the *armées* were is not easy to assess. Sneered at by many as 'butter and cheese soldiers', since so many of them concentrated on searching for hoarded food, most of their members were between thirty and fifty years old, unfit and ill-disciplined. The departmental *armées*, unlike that of Paris, also included some of the very poor and some foreigners, who perhaps had more interest in pay and loot than Revolutionary principles. However, despite cases of indiscipline and pillage, especially of food and drink, they were not in general either criminal or excessively brutal, although in certain circumstances they could be hard and cruel and certainly were much hated by the peasants they bullied [**doc. 15**]. The most extreme example, the grisly and psychopathic *armée Marat* at Nantes, could at least claim the justification of being almost swamped in a sea of counter-revolution and having seen the bodies of their comrades obscenely mutilated by the Chouans (**161**, i, ch. 5; **141**, ch. 4; **189**, ch. 9).

The *armées* never managed to enforce the *Maximum* completely, but they did largely succeed in ensuring supplies of grain and bread for Paris, though they had less success with butter, eggs and meat [**doc. 16**]. They also had a good record on the collection of church bells and gold or silver plate for the war effort. These achievements occurred in the absence of any genuine regional economic policy. Again, the *armées* were the chief agents in the rather unsystematic dechristianisation campaign, though here too they alienated the countryside, especially its women. That the Republican soldier was fed and clothed in the Year II and that victory was achieved at Fleurus owed a good deal to the efforts of the *armées révolutionnaires*. Repressive missions, the most crucial being that of the Parisian *armée* at Lyon, and the mass arrests were less useful, in that they were costly and impossible to mount without regular troops, as well as intensifying royalism, pushing many more into counter-revolution and creating friction with local authorities (**161**, ii, chs 1–4) [**doc. 15**].

The Revolutionary government had supported the creation of the *armées* in the autumn of 1793 with considerable reluctance, foreseeing problems of control and co-ordination of their operations. Essentially forced on the government by militant *sans culotte* opinion, the *armées* did not last long. Those in the departments were abolished by the law of 14 Frimaire (4 December 1793), the Parisian army lasting until 7 Germinal (27 March 1794). The *armées* were abolished as part of the government's policy of putting a brake on the anarchic Terror and the dechristianisation campaign by enforcing the authority of central governmental institutions like the C.P.S. and the C.G.S. against local initiatives and 'indiscipline', which, it alleged, led to 'federalism'; in other words, the slipping-away of control of the Revolution from the politicians in Paris (**161**, ii, ch. 7). The Parisian *armée* in particular seemed likely to become a tool of the Hébertists* and 'military plotters'.

At a local level, an essential part of the structure of the Terror was the network of revolutionary committees (*comités révolutionnaires*) and watch committees (*comités de surveillances*) officially established in every commune from 21 March 1793, although many had come into existence after the *journée* of 10 August 1792. Each committee had twelve elected members and assisted the 'constituted authorities' – the districts and the municipalities – in implementing Revolutionary measures. These were often at a rather mundane level: issuing *certificats de civisme* and arrest warrants, visiting prisons, destroying such signs of 'feudalism' as the fleur-de-lys on public buildings, arresting those who possessed pictures of the royal family and generally trying to enforce Revolutionary orthodoxy as they conceived it, and so far as it could be enforced on a reluctant and partly uncomprehending populace. The revolutionary committees were the cornerstone of the edifice of repression, having been mobilised against Federalism and the consequent breakdown of the local-government system [**doc. 23**]. Usually their members were composed of the active minority in the urban revolutionary clubs. As with other agencies of the Terror, their members were more lethargic and thin on the ground in rural areas, when they existed there at all (**188**, ch. 3; **191**, ch. 5).

Equally essential to the operation of Revolutionary justice, itself an expression of the 'vengeance of the people' and the determination of the government, were the Revolutionary tribunals. That of Paris was rapidly expanded after September 1793, condemning 177 out of 395 accused up to 30 December. Those in the departments were, on the other hand, often dilatory, being composed of painstaking *ancien régime* lawyers; the one at Metz executed nobody before the end of November. To speed up Revolutionary justice, extraordinary tribunals were set up without juries in various counter-revolutionary localities, such as Brest, Nancy, Lyon, Marseilles, Nîmes and Toulon (**189**, ch. 9; **192**, ch. 8) [**docs 19, 20, 21**].

The tribunals operated in the same anarchic conditions as the *armées révolutionnaires*, having to compete with military commissions and army tribunals which pronounced swift death sentences. After 14 Frimaire priority was awarded to the Paris tribunal, but others survived and were reinvigorated in the spring of 1794. Justice dispensed by the Revolutionary tribunals was speedy and without right of appeal. Javogues, the ultra-revolutionary *représentant* in the Loire, felt that twenty-four hours between the arrest and burial of a *suspect* was ample time, but his view was shaped by the fact that the tribunal in the Loire department was one of the most slow-moving and pettifogging (**191**, ch. 9).

Much of the impetus behind the Terror stemmed from economic motives: the desire of the government to mobilise productive resources in order to feed the urban population and supply the armies. After December 1793 the C.P.S. had considerable success, but during the period of the anarchic Terror there was no real soundly-based economic programme, if only because genuine central government hardly existed. The massive efforts of the Food Committee (*Commission des subsistances*) to encourage new agricultural techniques brought only limited results. Requisitioning tended to be piecemeal as some areas were stripped of their stocks of food and were themselves obliged to undertake requisitions among their weaker neighbours, while other areas were hardly touched (**162**). There was no general rationing system; hoarding and black marketeering continued to flourish. Farmers upset by the *Maximum* and by the attacks of the despised *armées révolutionnaires*, tended to hold on to their stocks of food at a time of such political uncertainty. Local taxes on the rich did little to mitigate a growing budget deficit, although the situation improved with a forced loan graduated on income, which was combined with the consolidation of the national debt. Certainly there was no serious attempt to transform the basic economic structure of society in a Revolution which was basically concerned with political power and the moulding of character, culture and social relations (**201**, introduction).

The Revolutionary government was trying to mount a war effort which, by demanding the participation of *all* citizens and national resources, foreshadowed the claims of twentieth-century states. It did so with only the limited resources of a pre-industrial society, but nevertheless it achieved a striking measure of success. A politicised and Revolutionary army was created, which had faith in the cause of the Republic against its enemies, a faith which made it a daunting antagonist. The *levée en masse* raised a nation in arms against foreign rulers and imbued it with a desire to 'liberate' and 'educate' subject peoples. Military service became the ultimate expression of patriotic enthusiasm, as well as providing for many a convenient ladder of social mobility. Although army commanders were still *ancien régime* nobles, a new, mobile citizen army gave opportunities to young officers unthinkable in the armies of the *ancien régime*, where those promoted from the ranks could never rise higher than lieutenant. Despite a good deal of insubordination and desertion, the French army proved a formidable fighting force by the spring of 1794, not least because of its ability to advance rapidly in columns, as opposed to lines (**188**, ch. 4; **109**, ch. 2). To supply the new army, France became something of a vast military workshop, organised by the indefatigable Carnot and the commissioners of war, who put out contracts, fixed wages, enforced industrial discipline and brought the knowledge of scientists to bear on war production. Popular enthusiasm for the war effort was exemplified by the campaign to extract saltpetre for gunpowder. Over 6,000 workshops were opened and a ninefold increase in production achieved. The Terror was a product of war and a means of winning it, and partly designed to extend the popular enthusiasm evident in Paris and the northern frontier regions to the markedly less enthusiastic west and south. This was what really mattered to the Revolutionary government; and in the end the war was won (**189**, chs 6–10) [**doc. 23**].

## Terrorists and Counter-Terrorists

Members of the institutions of the Terror were an extremely varied group of men, by no means all of whom were militants. Generally speaking, they were townsmen from lowland areas, for the Terror was very much an urban phenomenon. Rural districts and towns in mountainous and forested country tended to be either counter-revolutionary or indifferent. Those involved in the machinery of the Terror followed a variety of occupations and formed no cohesive social group: this was true even of the Paris *sans culottes*. In the capital as in the provinces, the very poor and the 'floating' population played no part, although the latter provided large numbers of recruits for the army (**168**). In the Year II (September 1793–September 1794), 26.2 per cent of members of Paris civil committees lived off private incomes, whilst over 60 per cent of the more popularly recruited revolutionary committees were skilled craftsmen or shopkeepers. Provincial *terroristes** were more often than not men of some financial standing. Occupying a post cost money, except in the regularly-paid *armées révolutionnaires*, and salaries were always well in arrears. Popular societies and clubs usually stipulated entrance fees and demanded not only literacy but also a considerable amount of a member's time. Certainly in the Loire department, terrorists cannot be equated with the Paris *sans culottes*, for the *menu peuple* were almost entirely excluded (**191**, ch. 11). Neither were they the upper crust of local society. What the Terror did was to bring to the fore men who had already participated in public life, but not at a very high level. Now they had a chance to eject old ruling groups and dominate the localities.

In Amiens, Bordeaux, Nancy and Toulouse, a new political class emerged during the Revolution, composed of merchants, manufacturers, artisans and shopkeepers, while the Terror gave countless opportunities to former 'marginal' men like innkeepers and schoolteachers (**201**, chs 5–6). At the same time, personal feuds and family antagonisms were not the least of the motives of the terrorists at the local level; nor was the desire for office and employment. The Terror gave many men a heady taste for power and access to occupations which had previously been denied them. Jean-Baptiste Lacombe, for example, began life as the mere second son of a humble Toulouse tailor, but became a schoolteacher. By the age of thirty-three he was the all-powerful president of the Military Commission at Bordeaux, responsible for running the Terror there.

While the Terror gave men a chance to rise from obscurity to positions of power and authority, in general terms it involved a transfer of political influence from the upper to the lower echelons of *ancien régime* society. Whatever their social background, however, militant terrorists were fervent republicans and democrats, masters of Revolutionary rhetoric who distrusted great wealth and high status. Yet such distrust was not based upon class antagonism. There were rich cotton masters and property owners, as well as artisans and shopkeepers, in the revolutionary societies of Lille; conversely, many moderates or counter-revolutionaries came from the same social groups as their opponents. Indeed, in some cases they came from the same families (**162**; **191**, ch. 11). Militant terrorism was more an individual than a class characteristic. Most of the terrorists were not very young – often between thirty-five and forty – and included both violent, unstable men and amiable *bon bougres* ('good chaps') with little taste for large-scale repression.

The factors which inclined men to support the Terror varied to the point of incalculability. Some became terrorists for reasons of self-defence in areas of counter-revolutionary or Federalist revolt; others were motivated by ties of blood, marriage, friendship, business relationships and neighbourhood loyalties. Yet others took their chance to pay off old scores. Above all, however, there was the motive of political beliefs, often independent of social background. Those who were enthusiastic democratic republicans and followed Rousseau in believing that government could create and mould a new people and a better society became most deeply involved in the Terror.

Yet political beliefs and attitudes often accompanied lesser motives. The chance to escape from a drab existence played its part in the careers of men like Javogues, Carrier and Carnot. The Revolution briefly licensed the anti-social temperament. One example is Nicholas Guénot of Voutenay in the Yonne department. Born into a family of impoverished rural labourers and lumbermen in 1754, he possessed a turbulent and aggressive character, deeply resenting the power of the local rich farmers and timber merchants. Drawn to Paris and various jobs there, Guénot quickly gained an unsavoury reputation. In 1776 he enrolled in the brutal and violent Paris-based French Guards regiment, but was dishonourably discharged seven years later after being constantly court-martialled and confined to military prisons. The Revolution presented him with a golden opportunity to combine ruthless advancement with vengeance. Within three years he had carved out a career for himself in the Revolutionary police bureaucracy as spy, informer and prison clerk, before becoming a police inspector. Late in 1793, at the age of 39, his brutal diligence gained him a post as full-time agent of the Committee of General Security.

But Guénot received most satisfaction from repressive missions to his native department, where he took the opportunity of denouncing the rich timbermen and farmers he had despised as a youth. After thoroughly enjoying the Terror and the chance for vengeance, he was dismissed for embezzlement in the spring of 1794. Probably because of his numerous criminal contacts, he was reinstated in the police and the underworld until again convicted of corruption in 1800 and sentenced to exile in his native village – the cruellest fate for any former terrorist. Back in Voutenay he was greeted with a mixture of fear and loathing by villagers as brutal and vindictive as himself. He was beaten up, driven out to live in the woods and generally ostracised. He died in 1832 at the age of 78, having had to suffer three decades of hostility and abuse for his brief enjoyment of the fruits of power (**198**). While there were many violent men like Guénot, other terrorists were former priests or dull and obscure provincial lawyers who constantly trimmed their sails to the prevailing political wind; or they were minor officials who took their chance of quick profits from government confiscations and contracts (**199**; **164**, ch. 3). In the countryside the Revolution and Terror tended to be supported by the independent richer peasant proprietors who saw their chance to strike at their old enemies: parish priests, *seigneurs* and rich outsiders.

The sources of counter-terrorism were equally varied; indeed the choice of Terror or counter-revolution was sometimes almost accidental. The counter-terror was essentially local and individual, for it lacked any national programme and drew its strength from habit and tradition, especially in the violent south of France. There were many men who were apathetic, although the Republic classed the indifferent with counter-revolutionaries [**doc. 20**]. Such men were often able to ignore the Terror and live completely outside it, for the government of the Year II lacked the resources of a Stalin or a Hitler, having, in Cobb's phrase, 'to rely on a man on a horse'. Some lived in the mountains, woods or other inaccessible areas; some were brigands and bandits who carried on with their daily round of robbery and grisly murder. Nor were the very poor much involved in the Terror, except in so far as they were its victims (**248**). Many people, especially in the Midi, were counter-revolutionary because of local pride and resentment of Paris and its high-flown Revolutionary slogans (**164**, introd., ch. 1; **192**; **142**). Women were frequently hostile to the Revolution because of the damage it did to the Church, the family and the shopping basket (**176**).

## The Effects of the Terror

The most striking effect of the Terror was the increase in government repression. Before 1789 people were used to seeing criminals branded, tortured and broken on the wheel – a horrific process whereby the victim's bones were smashed with an iron bar and the mutilated corpse displayed on a cartwheel. Since its beginning, the Revolution had been shaped by violence; but such violence had tended to come from angry crowds rather than the Revolutionary government. What was new after the beginning of the Year II (September 1793) was that the Terror was organised and became for the first time a deliberate policy of government (**189**, ch. 2). Of course, it may well be that had this government repression not existed, more people would have been killed in popular outbursts of violence like the *bagarre de Nîmes* of May 1790. Below the elegant surface of high society, the French people were brutal and bloodthirsty.

Before the fall of the Robespierrists in Thermidor (July 1794), something like 30,000 people had been killed by the official Terror. Perhaps as many more had been murdered or lynched without trial or official record, with up to a further 10,000 dying in custody. Such a number is small by twentieth-century standards. But it horrified European opinion, even though the same number were killed in a few weeks in Ireland in the rising of 1798, a country with only a sixth of France's population, while about 45,000 were slaughtered in a single day in Warsaw on 4 November 1794 (**265**, ch. 11). Rather than the nobles and clergy of legend – who actually lost 9 per cent and 6 per cent of their respective numbers – the majority of victims were ordinary men and women from the lower ranks of society who had opted for Revolution or counter-revolution at the wrong time (**194**, chs 2, 5). Many of these died in the stinking, overcrowded goals. The most barbarous aspect of the Terror was repression against counter-revolutionaries after Republican victories in the Civil War. At Lyon, Fouché and Collot d'Herbois had hundreds of suspects killed by cannon fire and blasted into open graves [**doc. 15**]. At Nantes, Carrier condoned the *noyades* (drownings) when about 2,000 prisoners were bound tight in holed barges and left to sink in the icy waters of the Loire; their bodies washed up on the tidal banks for weeks afterwards (**189**, chs 7, 9).

Such extreme atrocities took place in counter-revolutionary areas, where royalists, Vendéans and Chouans had themselves killed Republicans by barbarous methods. A Republican wife could return home to find her husband's genitals nailed to the door (**141**, ch. 5). Over 70 per cent of executions under the Terror took place in limited areas of the west and south-east. Paris was far outranked by the provinces so far as the number of victims was concerned. In fact the region around Paris, plus the central areas of France, suffered least. Only the war zones on the frontiers and the vulnerable coasts could rival the areas of civil war in the intensity of the Terror (**194**, ch. 3).

The largest number of executions under the Terror took place during the period of the 'anarchic' Terror between October 1793 and January 1794, but such intensity of repression was modified by geographical variations. Even in areas of repression there could be towns and villages hardly touched by the Terror. Indeed some places were hardly touched by the Revolution, let alone the Terror. The village of Authieux, near Rouen, had 289 inhabitants in 1789. 'No political events between 1789 and 1793 troubled the quiet life of the parish, sheltered from the general movement which transformed the nation' (**195**). The only approach to anything like

Revolutionary crisis in Authieux was resentment at the requisitioning of grain to feed nearby Rouen.

Like Authieux, the little community of Pourrain in the Yonne department, with its 1,200 inhabitants, failed to show much interest in the Revolution, varying between indifference and positive resistance. Daily life hardly changed and attempts by *commissaires* from Auxerre to recruit for the army and force farmers to send grain to market at a time of inflation met with little success. Pourrain acknowledged the Revolution only when forced to do so by urban interlopers, and after Thermidor it swiftly cleared away all relics of the Revolution before fully restoring the Church and the cross-roads Calvary. France was full of such rural communities for whom the Revolution meant pompous officials trying to disturb a deeply-entrenched traditional culture (**252**, conclusion).

It is far from easy to summarise the effects of the Terror on the population as a whole. There were those who paid with their lives; there were those who were unaffected. Men from the same area and same social group could find either opportunity or disaster during the year II of the Republic. A more meaningful approach is to ask how the Terror affected a particular region (**191**; **192**; **144**; **179**). Nevertheless, some attempt can be made at generalisation. Revolution and Terror did little or nothing for the eight million very poor, about a third of the population of France in 1790, though neither politically nor ideologically significant. Local militants on revolutionary committees tended to be anxious to protect property and preserve public order, as well as possessing a parsimonious attitude towards charity, based on a concept of the 'deserving' (that is, 'Revolutionary') poor. Destitute women and runaway and delinquent children were hounded mercilessly. Adequate treatment of the poor was one of the most conspicuous failures of the Revolutionary regimes. Hospitals, schools and charities were hard-hit by Revolutionary legislation. Nineteen of the forty-three hospitals in the department of the Hérault were forced to close down, while in Grenoble all the government succeeded in doing was to wreck most of the existing arrangements for assisting the poor.

Attacks on the religious orders robbed hospitals and schools of trained staff. At the same time the abolition of feudal dues and rents undermined their finances: the hospital of Saint-André in Bordeaux, for example, had received most of its income from feudal dues presented by rich patrons. Moreover, war brought disproportionate suffering to the poor, for they bore the main burden of disrupted trade, military recruitment and grain requisitions

(**247**). Revolutionary decrees on poverty were nullified by a clumsily bureaucratic military apparatus, by ignorance of local circumstances and practice and, above all, by the fact that inflation, war and blockade absorbed the money needed to implement a centralised and state-controlled system of welfare. In large towns like Marseille, Bordeaux and Lyon, the problem of the urban poor was particularly acute and their lot undoubtedly deteriorated after 1789. For the poor, then, the French Revolution and Terror proved disastrous, though that was not the intention of the Revolutionary governments (**192**, ch. 11; **249**; **250**).

A Revolution so keen on the rights of man hardly gave a thought to those of women. Total war, implying large armies and movements of workers into war industries, meant increased mobility and more sexual opportunities for men. Married women were increasingly deserted; so were single pregnant girls. Many of them were forced into prostitution, itself not the least of the expanding war industries (**177**; **164**, ch. 8). Such changes threatened the stability of the family at a time when dearth and high prices meant long queues for stale, putrid food and impossible strain on the family budgets of working women in the towns [**doc. 20**]. Meanwhile a crisis in trade and the collapse of the luxury industries undermined women's employment. The woman who had proudly urged her sons to join the army, who spouted Revolutionary slogans, who poured out venom against priests and *émigrés*, became soured by economic deprivation and desperate attempts to feed her family. She became 'ultimately the worn-out, disillusioned, starving hag who sank to her knees in Year III to demand pardon of an offended Christ' (**176**).

There is no doubt that the Terror gave men opportunities for upward social mobility. In some areas the Terror seems almost to have been operated solely by former wig-makers. Such men were normally town dwellers. If the Terror originated in the towns, then it created a good deal of antagonism in the countryside. What to townsmen, the educated, and heirs of the *philosophes* looked like a more enlightened way of ordering matters, seemed very different to peasants experiencing the consequences of enforcing *vertu** by requisitioning grain and suppressing local custom. A great deal of counter-revolutionary violence stemmed from a defence of local interests and traditional values against the consequences of applying a new revolutionary ideology which villagers found both alien and incomprehensible (**147**). Hence there was little love lost between the *sans culottes* on the one hand and the peasantry and inhabitants of small market towns on the other. Although some peasants profited from inflation and labour shortages, most of them disliked the manner in which townsmen operated the Terror to their own advantage: to feed themselves, to monopolise official posts, to evade conscription, and to get their hands on the confiscated wealth of the Church and *émigrés*. The urban classes, in response, accused 'grasping peasants' of deliberately attempting to starve the towns and obstruct the operation of the Terror, thereby encouraging the enemies of the Republic.

The dechristianisation campaign, which began in late 1792 and returned in more intense form in the autumn of 1793, also proved divisive. Churches were stripped of their valuables, to be fed into the war machine. The churches themselves were often turned into workshops, barracks, arsenals or stables. But there was more to it than the obvious need to sustain the war effort. Their rejection of Christianity was one of the chief ways in which the Revolutionaries announced their break with the French and European past. The new regime was grounded in reason and the natural rights of man, not the revelation of God: hence the formal ceremonies where statues, relics, roadside calvaries and other sacred objects were destroyed, and the names of streets, squares, inn signs and towns purged of all references to the Christian or 'feudal' past. Some of the impetus for dechristianisation stemmed from the failure of the 'constitutional' Church after 1790. Yet custom and habit carried such weight in the countryside that the Revolution was unable to change attitudes as thoroughly as it desired. Religion remained powerful in rural France, especially among women; this was one of the reasons for the fierce anti-feminism of the popular movement. Urban *sans culottes* developed cults of Marat, Lepeletier and Chalier, 'martyrs' murdered by counter-revolutionaries, which involved a secularised political version of Catholic liturgy and imagery. But these cults, and a similar one of Rousseau, remained largely confined to a minority of urban militants and helped deepen hostility to the Revolution in much of the countryside (**206**; **202**, ch. 10) [**doc. 14**].

Nor did the subsequent cults of Reason and the Supreme Being do much to mitigate the effects of Revolutionary assaults on the Church, for the iconoclasm and vandalism of the dechristianisation campaign during the winter of 1793–94 sowed further divisions in the country rather than contributing to national unity by erasing a 'corrupt ' past based on superstition (**204**; **209**; **210**). A few village artisans may have welcomed the Terror, but the majority of peasants were glad to see the fall of Robespierre and his followers in Thermidor and the end of the 'despotism of liberty' in 1794–95.

## 'Saint Maximilien'

The period of the Great Terror from September 1793 to July 1794 is most closely associated with the name of Robespierre, the most widely-known and prominent member of the Committee of Public Safety, although he never controlled it. While his personality remains an enigma, his public life has aroused prolonged debate – a debate about his motives, intentions and influence which has now been going on for 200 years and looks like continuing for ever. At the time of the bicentennial celebrations there were determined efforts to have a memorial to him or street named after him in Paris by a group which pointed out that Robespierre, the so-called incarnation of Terror, sent far fewer men to their deaths than, for example, Georges Clemenceau after the mutinies in the First-World-War French army. No statesman has been so grotesquely adulated and maligned by both contemporaries and posterity (**236**, part ii). Historians of the Right see Robespierre as an austere tyrant, whose alleged personal ascendancy in late 1793 and early 1794 proved the antithesis of democracy and brought the Revolution to ruin and collapse in an orgy of executions. He has been accused of dictatorship, or desiring to create a personal cult, of employing the Great Terror solely and cynically for the purpose of perpetuating himself in power (**238**). Irritated by his self-righteousness and incorruptibility, writers have depicted him as intolerant of any opposition to his own views and tactics.

Generally reviled in the nineteenth century, Robespierre's reputation was rehabilitated by Albert Mathiez, for whom, as for so many Jacobins and *sans culottes* in 1792 and 1793, he was 'this saint of democracy' (**212**, chs 1, 3). Since Mathiez, historians have disagreed on their assessment of Robespierre; so have French politicians. The bicentenary of his birth in 1958 provoked fisticuffs in the Paris municipal council (**239**, foreword). Marxist historians are similarly divided. Some see him as pointing the way towards socialism (**223**); others are unable to forgive him for attacking the *enragés* and Hébertists and accuse him of betraying the interests of the people in 1794 when he destroyed the popular societies and imposed a *maximum* on wages, even though it could not be widely applied (**214**; **215**). When he was executed in Thermidor, the poor Parisian workers (*bras nus*) shouted, 'There goes the [wages] *Maximum* into the basket'. Despite the hostility of Marx, who saw Robespierre as more of a symptom than an agent of misguided Jacobinism and Terror, George Rudé, himself a Marxist, has portrayed

'Saint Maximilien' as a sincere political and social democrat (**236**, part iii).

To some degree certainly, Robespierre was the creature of circumstances, for whom Terror and 'the despotism of liberty' was a necessary response to war, treachery, internal rebellion and the dangers of a 'military plot' (**212**, ch. 3; **237**, chs 7, 8). But there was more to it than that. Robespierre was a visionary who stood for the creation of a new moral order in which service to the community would replace *ancien régime* aristocratic frivolity and bourgeois greed, and where the government would be responsive and responsible to the whole (male) nation. Hence the Revolutionary government of the Year II aimed at perpetuating the existence of democratic rule and the life of the French Republic, even if democracy hardly existed in practice [**doc. 21**]. This vision was one shared at the time by many Jacobins, including the even more abstract Saint-Just (**189**, ch. 11; **216**; **240**, ch. 11). France would become not merely a democratic republic, but a republic of virtue (*vertu*). The end justified the means; to bring about such a glorious future justified the Terror. So Robespierre, the former opponent of the death penalty, condoned, in the spring of 1794, the wholesale execution of people who posed little threat to anyone, whereas in late 1793 he had tried to prevent the execution of Marie Antoinette and the Girondin leaders. In his most memorable speech, delivered before the Convention on 5 February 1794, Robespierre exclaimed: 'If the aim of popular government in peacetime is virtue, then the aim of popular government at a time of Revolution is virtue and terror at one and the same time: virtue, without which terror is disastrous; terror, without which virtue is impotent'.

It is difficult to see Robespierre as other than a tragic figure, for his attempt to blend together Rousseauist political philosophy with the practical leadership of the Revolutionary government and vicious in-fighting of factional politics ended in failure and early death. He was very much a man of the eighteenth-century Enlightenment, convinced of the supremacy of spiritual values and the eternal laws of reason. In his eyes, only the application of fundamental moral principles in government could provide the antidote for political corruption and bring about social happiness. Robespierre, in other words, saw politics as a branch of ethics. His basic political ideas were taken from Rousseau's *Social Contract* (1762), as indeed were those of many Jacobins and *sans culottes*, though in a more indirect and unsystematic manner (**86**, chs 8–12). Like Rousseau, Robespierre regarded the people in general, as opposed to particular individuals, as naturally good and capable of *vertu*. By 'virtue' he meant love of country (*la patrie*) and the identification of public and private interests. For Robespierre, always instinctively a moral crusader, the 'nation' and the 'people' were interchangeable terms, since the nation was simply the practical expression of the sovereignty of the people: a Republic of free men with equality of rights. The individual must be transformed into a tiny part of a greater whole (**216**; **213**; **217**).

Before entering the Committee of Public Safety in August 1793 Robespierre had achieved a formidable reputation as a political tactician, orator, debater and a champion of the underprivileged. He had defended the liberty of the press, argued in favour of a democratic franchise, and defended generally-despised minority groups such as Jews and negro slaves. He had also urged as much direct democracy as possible, insisting in 1792 that the popular societies of the *sans culottes* were necessary to diffuse 'public spirit' and experience of democratic politics. What eventually separated him from the *enragés*, the Hébertists and many others at the grass roots of the popular movement was that he tended to see equality in purely political terms. Like his colleagues in the C.P.S. (with the possible exception of Collot d'Herbois) Robespierre had little intimate knowledge of the lives of the common people, still less of the poor. As Soboul pointed out, Robespierre, although a sincere democrat, 'felt ill at ease among the people. A man of the Assembly and the Jacobin Club, he lacked any real feeling for mass action' (**214**).

Following Rousseau, Robespierre disliked great inequalities of wealth and approved of diatribes against the rich, but his own economic ideas were primitive and unsystematic, while he was too much a product of the educated bourgeoisie to reject property as the basis of the social order. Even so, his draft Declaration of Rights in 1793, more radical than the final version, reveals his willingness to go further in the direction of economic equality than the more moderate members of the Convention. However, the fact that so many of the *menu peuple* cared more for the price of bread and the level of wages than for the life of Republican virtue irked him. Robespierre regarded the two *enragés* Roux and Varlet as little more than unprincipled ruffians who exploited the people by appealing to the base demands of their bellies (**214**; **236**, ch. 2).

After the autumn of 1793 the exigencies of power caused Robespierre to modify his Rousseauist views; indeed to go beyond them. From being a stern critic of the powers of government, he became an advocate of the supremacy of the Convention and the Committee of Public Safety as embodiments of the infallible 'general will'. In his speech of 25 December 1793 (the Nativity was ignored), Robespierre admitted that constitutional principles could not be implemented literally and that a government 'Revolutionary until the peace' had to wield more authority than one in peacetime [**doc. 21**]. Yet the purged Convention was clearly representative only of a minority of Montagnards, while even the popular movement had begun to fragment. In his desire to consolidate the Revolutionary government, Robespierre was instrumental in reducing the role and influence of the popular societies after December 1793 and clearing the way for the supremacy of the monolithic government machine. He fully supported the brake which the C.P.S. put on the 'anarchic' Terror and on local initiative by the Law of 14 Frimaire (14 December 1793). This firmly founded the central Revolutionary dictatorship by preventing the *représentants en mission* delegating their powers without prior approval from Paris; by abolishing the provincial *armées révolutionnaires*; by putting departmental, district and communal institutions under the inspection of 'national agents' of the C.P.S. and C.G.S.; and by forbidding any independent taxes or loans at a local level. Thus the Republic was given a more rigorous and powerful bureaucracy than any eighteenth-century monarchy (**1**, doc. 53; **3**, doc. 118). Moreover, Robespierre was the main opponent of the 'anarchic' dechristianisation campaign, for he had always supported religious toleration and regarded atheism as aristocratic and counter-revolutionary. Dechristianisers, in his opinion, must be enemies of the people because of the way they sowed division and stirred antagonisms.

So far as Robespierre was concerned, government dictatorship and Terror were vital to the safety of the Republic. If it were necessary to use violence against the enemies of the people, then his legalistic mind preferred judicial violence by the government rather than the indiscriminate and uncontrolled mayhem of popular insurrections (*émeutes*) like the September massacres of 1792. Bound up with his conception of the Terror and Republican virtue was commitment to the war. Patriotism was the other side of the coin of virtue. The war which France was waging must be one for principle rather than for gain; a war for justice and liberty rather than conquest. But a war against tyrants must be fought to the death. By arguing on these lines, Robespierre came close to accepting the war ideology for which he had denounced the Girondins in 1792. Yet the aggressive nationalism which accompanied French victories, plus the increasing exploitation of occupied foreign territories, made the concept of war for liberty and justice look ever more threadbare [**doc. 18**].

In a situation of rival minorities, there was so much evident corruption and factional struggle that Robespierre more and more came to see the general will as an 'ideal' will that had, if necessary, to be imposed on people. The 'people' became in fact a smaller and smaller minority. Early in the Revolution, Robespierre had used 'people' to mean the non-privileged groups. By 1794 the 'people' meant merely those who supported the Revolutionary government. So the ideal will emerged from a small minority of virtuous republicans and patriots: the C.P.S. and its Jacobin supporters. Hence the need for purges of all who spoke against the Revolutionary dictatorship, whatever their previous record of revolutionary orthodoxy.

While his final aims remain rather mysterious, there is little reason to doubt that he valued political liberty and regarded the Revolutionary dictatorship as a temporary expedient to deal with an extraordinary crisis. Although Robespierre can be regarded, in Aulard's phrase, as 'the high priest of political orthodoxy', he was not the personal tyrant portrayed by his enemies at Thermidor. He exercised no dominant authority in either the Jacobin Club or in the Committee of Public Safety: Barère, Carnot and Prieur signed many more decrees. Nor does he bear sole responsibility for the intensive Terror of 1794. While he agreed that enemies of the people deserved death, he revoked a good many arrests and sentences, and opposed the execution of Danton. He was never as severe as the members of the Committee of General Security or his merciless young colleague Saint-Just, the 'angel of death' (**237**, ch. 8).

During the spring and summer of 1794 the government launched a massive propaganda campaign, which included strict control of the press and the theatre, elaborate festivals of Liberty, Equality, Justice and Amity, as well as the cult of the Supreme Being (**202**, ch. 5). These were designed to promote a civic religion of humanity which, hoped Robespierre, would wean the people from both the 'superstitions of Catholicism' and the 'immorality' of the cult of Reason, thus bringing about social regeneration and loyalty to the Revolutionary government [**doc. 22**]. Nature was the true priest of the Supreme Being; its temple was the universe. J.-L. David, the leading neo-classical artist of the age, was called into design impressive tableaux and scenic effects for the civic festivals. It soon became apparent, however, that the reign of Rousseauist virtue was inoperable. Officially-supported puritan rigour of conduct, serving as the basis of a new moral order, had little appeal outside Jacobin and government circles, especially when the Republican armies began to push back the enemy.

In the event, the Revolutionary government soon lost touch with the masses and came to represent no specific interest but that of its own leaders and officials. By the early months of 1794 it had come to believe that it could operate the Terror and win the war without the support of the popular movement and turn the machinery of Terror against those, both on the right and the left, who voiced any criticism of the Revolutionary dictatorship. The popular societies were therefore proscribed and *sans culotte* artillery units absorbed into the armies on the frontier, well away from Paris (**237**, ch. 18; **161**, ii, book iv, ch. 2). Such a conflict between the government and what it dismissed as 'the factions' was not so much a class struggle, though it contained elements of one, as a conflict about power, jobs, patronage and influence. The *sans culotte* idea of direct democracy, with the people of Paris possessing their own armed force and popular committees with police powers, proved unacceptable to the two great Committees. Popular protest was therefore reduced to the level of riots and demonstrations. Militants were bought off by being offered lucrative jobs in the bureaucracy. The result of this dismissal of the popular movement was the increasing isolation of the government and the spread of apathy and indifference throughout the country. As Saint-Just, who aimed at transforming France into a new Sparta, complained: 'The Revolution is frozen-solid'.

Beneath the surface of rhetoric by Revolutionary leaders, stage management by David and the 701 new political songs which appeared in 1794, there was precious little virtue (**255**). Hunger and misery in Paris were rivalled only by the scale of gambling and prostitution. Such a ferment seemed to threaten the propertied classes and the stability of the Republic. In Ventôse (February–March 1794) the government turned on the 'factions'. Hébert and his colleagues, it was alleged, were fomenting popular discontent from their bases in the Commune, the Cordeliers Club and the War Office. In fact only the *section Marat* ward of the city, in which the Cordeliers was situated, seemed prepared for insurrection. Such ultra-revolutionaries, claimed Robespierre and the leading Jacobins, were attempting to undermine the government by the 'anarchic' aims of dechristianisation, rigorous price controls and death for dishonest merchants and traders. Hébert, Vincent, Momoro and the heads of the Parisian *armée révolutionnaire*, Ronsin and Mazuell, were

101

arrested, quickly tried, and executed, marking the commencement of a campaign against 'extremism'.

Although the *sans culottes* were stunned when *Père Duchesne* went to the guillotine, they did nothing. Anxiety and shocked silence replaced patriotic exaltation and Revolutionary fervour in the Paris *sections*. As issue 111 of *Le Vieux Cordelier* put it: 'You had to show joy at the death of your friend or relative unless you wanted to risk death yourself' (**96,** ch. 9). There was in fact no Hébertist party with a genuine alternative programme and the so-called Hébertists were men using the popular movement to further their own ambition to gain lucrative posts and patronage. But most *sans culottes* viewed the execution of the Hébertists as yet another step in the repression of the popular movement and a denial of the right of insurrection (**161,** book ii, part iii). By acting against Paris and the popular movement, the C.P.S. seemed to be acting against the Revolution itself. Partly to forestall charges of being reactionary, the government turned on Danton and the 'Indulgents'. They were accused of moderation, of desiring to end the war, of connections with foreign plotters and of shady financial dealings. They were executed on 16 Germinal (5 April) after Danton had spoken so vigorously in his defence that the jury had to be bribed and threatened [**doc. 25**].

If the fall the Hébertists marked the end of the *sans culottes* as a political force, the fall of the Dantonists* frightened many moderate deputies in the Convention, of which the Dantonists were members (**187**). Such deputies, so afraid of arrest that they slept away from home, as well as the propertied classes in general, had earlier been upset by the laws of Ventose, whereby Saint-Just proposed that the property of *suspects* be confiscated by the state and the proceeds given to the poor. Lists of both suspects and poor were to be drawn up by local authorities. This was partly a political manoeuvre, aimed at purchasing the loyalty of the *sans culottes* to a regime which was reducing them to political nullity. The proposals were also intended to calm growing peasant unrest. In fact very little was done in a systematic way to implement the laws of Ventôse. There were some piecemeal confiscations in about thirty departments, but administration proved too chaotic and the will too absent for any large-scale transfers of wealth. Few politicians saw the Terror as the opportunity for launching a permanent social revolution (**226**). By raising fears for the security of property, fears already aroused by a forced loan on the rich, without doing much to meet the demands of the poor, the Revolutionary government satisfied nobody and deepened hostilities on both sides (**188,** ch. 5).

# 7 Thermidor

The great Committee of Public Safety survived the execution of the Dantonists* by a mere 113 days, for in the late spring and early summer of 1794 the Revolutionary government became more isolated and resented as people wearied of the slaughter. Many began to see the government as either the personal dictatorship of the increasingly paranoid Robespierre, or that of the 'triumvirate' of Robespierre, Saint-Just and Couthon, the crippled deputy from the Auvergne. Both views lacked substance, but the fact that they were held is testimony to the growing atmosphere of suspicion and panic reminiscent of the Great Fear of 1789. Jacobin clubs in Paris and the provinces were in a state of confusion and frequently seethed with intrigue. The Revolutionary government still looked formidable on paper, but it broke down completely in some parts of France, like the Ardèche and the Var. The Paris *sans culottes* were angered by the food shortage and the refusal of the Commune to raise wages.

By this time Revolutionary government had become very much ruled by the bureaucrats. Government offices were full of men with a little education and a mere veneer of *civisme*. Militants were either imprisoned or rendered impotent by the bureaucratic mentality. Initiative was stifled at all levels below that of the great Committees; energy which had formerly gone into the 'anarchic Terror' now went into petty quarrels and personal intrigues between rival officials. In an atmosphere of fear and uncertainty, a dull conformity seemed the most judicious course to adopt. Government propaganda on behalf of *vertu* tended to encourage a defensive hypocrisy at the most, or plain boredom at the least, without doing much to diminish robbery, excess and a good deal of place-seeking and financial corruption. A general fear of 'foreign plots', 'prison plots' and assassinations, partly justified by the presence in Paris of large numbers of foreign spies and prisoners in insecure custody, led to the acceleration of Revolutionary 'justice'. The government seemed to be losing its nerve and falling apart.

Late in May, government panic was deepened by two attempts on Robespierre's life (**222**). The great Terror of June and July 1794 represented a frantic attempt to preserve itself by a government which felt the ground slipping beneath its feet. Over 2,500 died in the two months before 9 Thermidor (27 July), more than the total for the previous year (**189**, ch. 13). These executions were the work of the Paris tribunal, which by this time had a monopoly; even death was centralised. The tribunal was specifically charged with punishing 'enemies of the people', so widely defined that virtually anyone became vulnerable. More of them were from the higher ranks of society than in the Terror as a whole; 38 per cent of noble victims, 26 per cent of clerical ones, and almost half those from the richer bourgeoisie died in this short period.

By the Law of 22 Prairial (10 June 1794) the rights of the accused to have counsel and to call witnesses were whittled away to nothing, as the guillotine worked ever faster. Such a bloodbath, without apparent purpose, provoked a general reaction of fear and extreme tension, besides encouraging the belief that the Terror was no longer a means of preserving the Republic, but rather the instrument of political faction, a device for settling old scores and maintaining the government in power.

The atmosphere in Paris in June and July 1794 was a mixture of general moroseness and hostility to the Jacobin dictatorship. As its authority became increasingly discredited, even those who had hitherto been keen Republicans felt disoriented. Until the end of June victory in the war was still uncertain, but on the 26th came the triumph of the Republican armies at Fleurus, followed by their entry into Brussels on 8 July. Now that the armies were on the offensive, the Terror no longer had the justification of the needs of national defence. Many deputies who had been voicing their qualms about the Terror since the beginning of the year now made their views public. Meanwhile the machinery of Revolutionary government had practically come to a halt in the provinces. The hesitancy of local authorities encouraged reaction: liberty trees, which had been planted all over France as a potent symbol of Revolution, were uprooted; there were refusals to draw up lists of *suspects*. People had had more than enough of militancy and slaughter, preferring to return to the workbench, the shop, the family and the tavern (*cabaret*) (**188**, ch. 6).

Priests emerged from hiding to encourage resistance to the Terror. Many women, despairing of the Revolution after the privations it had brought them, sought consolation in Christianity, going on pilgrimages and, in some cases, working themselves up to such a pitch that they claimed to have witnessed miracles. The great festival of 'the Supreme Being' in Notre-Dame on 20 Prairial (8 June) did little to absorb this resurgence of religious feeling. On the contrary it led to suspicions that Robespierre aimed at his own deification (**202**, ch. 5). Economic distress was also rife in Paris, with a renewed food shortage leading to demands for higher wages. Yet the C.P.S. and the Paris Commune* issued a new *Maximum** on wages which would have involved starvation for many families. A carpenter, for example, would receive 3 *francs* 15 *sous*, instead of 8 *francs*. A labour agitation therefore took place which further widened the breach between the government and the common people in the towns (**223**; **96**, ch. 9). At the same time the peasantry was alienated by the erratic operation of the *Maximum* on grain and consumables.

Robespierre himself almost seemed to welcome political suicide. In a state of nervous exhaustion, he absented himself from the C.P.S. in June. The Committee itself began to come apart under the strain of constant internal divisions. Panic became vindictive. In the Convention, moderate members of the 'Plain' felt menaced as the great Terror increased momentum and the number of prisoners in the capital soared alarmingly (**222**). Such an atmosphere of apprehension provided a suitable environment for the flourishing of plots and rumours. The conspiracy to bring down Robespierre therefore had a good deal of tacit support. Many deputies had never forgiven the Montagnards for calling in the *sans culottes* to get rid of the Girondins on 2 June 1793. They had been willing to sanction the power of the great Committees only because of the seriousness of the national crisis, while still resenting the domination of the legislature by the executive (**22**; **24**, ch. 6). On 8 Thermidor (26 July 1794), Robespierre made his last speech in the Convention, denouncing the C.G.S. and the Treasury, denying that he was a dictator, pointing to the danger of a military plot and urging reconciliation. It availed him little, for next day his enemies closed in on him. Amid shouts of 'Down with the tyrant!' the Convention decreed the arrests of Robespierre, his brother Augustin, Saint-Just, Couthon and Le Bas. Robespierre fled to the *mairie*, the others being taken to prison, from which they soon escaped to join him, assuming that the *mairie* in the Hôtel de Ville would be defended by *sans culottes* and the National Guard. Declared outlaws, they were swiftly recaptured, Robespierre being shot (or shooting himself) in the jaw. Next day they were executed in the Place de la Révolution (now Place de la Concorde) with seventeen others; outlaws were not permitted a trial (**236**, part i; **237**, ch. 9). A force of

3,000 *sans culottes* had assembled in the Place de Grève on the evening of 9 Thermidor, but had failed to act decisively. Paris remained passive as Robespierre and his colleagues went to the guillotine, soon to be followed by nearly a hundred 'Robespierrists'. The more prosperous inhabitants of the capital, however, cheered as the bodies were dragged away to a ditch of quicklime.

To general relief, the personnel of the Revolutionary government was drastically purged and the machinery of Terror dismantled within a few weeks. Over 3,500 *suspects* were released from prison in August, intent on vengeance. The country passed into a determined and savage reaction against Montagnards and *terroristes* of all shades. Control of the Paris *sections* was seized by moderates, while the repulsive *jeunesse dorée* ('gilded youth'), gangs of pomaded and elaborately-dressed royalist youths, spearheaded a witch-hunt against Jacobins with a brutality that rivalled the Year II. The 'White Terror' of the Year III (September 1794–September 1795) frequently took the form of undisciplined murder gangs operating against terrorists in counter-revolutionary areas, especially the south-east. As many people were murdered in the south-east and the west of France between 1795 and 1803 as had perished during the Terror of the Year II. Many others took refuge in exile, or even suicide (**163**, book ii, part ii; **142**, ch. 3; **258**, ch. 7).

Inflation soared with the abandoning of economic controls, and continued high war expenditure led to still higher food prices. The poor became even worse off than they had been during the Year II. By contrast, the wealthy classes profited from inflation and speculation, throwing their money about on food ('lobster Thermidor'), *salons* and high fashion. Virtue, in short supply during the Jacobin Terror, was almost entirely absent in the general reaction against 'puritanism' which characterised the Thermidorian* regime. Half-hearted *sans cullote* risings, motivated primarily by sheer hunger among the genuine manual workers (*bras nus*), were put down by cannonfire in Germinal and Prairial (April and May) 1795, to be followed by savage repression. This left bitter memories, but there was to be no further popular rising in Paris until 1848 (**96**, ch. 10). From the autumn of 1795 until Napolean's *coup d'état* of Brumaire in November 1799, the conservative Republic was plagued by instability, as it oscillated between right and left under the Directory, trying to avoid the extremes of royalism and republican extremism by successive purges, with the aid of the army. By 1797 the government was so weak that it was clearly only a matter of time before the army dismissed the civilians and controlled the Republic.

# Part Four: Assessment

## 8 The French Revolution in Perspective

After two centuries, the French Revolution still divides the nation. It proved impossible to celebrate the bicentenary in 1989 with the same ease as Americans had done with their revolution or Australians the white settlement of their continent. There were fewer problems with the centenary of the Revolution, for in 1889 the quasi-Bonapartist General Boulanger had attempted to seize power and the claim that the principles of 1789 were those of liberty and progress evoked a sympathetic response, especially when the Third Republic proclaimed itself the natural successor to the Revolution. The 150th anniversary in 1939 was more problematic. The President of the Republic was opposed to celebrations, assuming that they would take the form of left-wing demonstrations with red flags and clenched fists. The French bourgeoisie were still shocked by the triumph of the Left at the 1936 elections and the formation of the Popular Front. Besides, more attention was focussed on international affairs and the threat from Germany. In the event, the general public remained largely unenthusiastic and most of the celebratory events were washed out by heavy rain.

In September 1981 François Mitterrand, the first Socialist President of the French Republic, set up various commissions to arrange the commemoration of the bicentenary of the French Revolution. He specified that these celebrations should reflect the place which the Revolution holds in the history of France and of the world. This was easier said than done, for deciding the final place of the Revolution turned out to be an impossible task. In France the Revolution is as much myth and legend as a set of events: a living issue which continues to divide the scholarly, the educated and the nostalgic. In Brittany in recent years, for example, plaques have been erected to victims of the Terror, including priests who died in defence of the Catholic faith. In the west of France, the *Souvenir Vendéen* club, founded in 1932, now has over two thousand royalist members. Right-wing parties and groups object to celebrating the Terror of 1792–94, which they see as the archetype of modern totalitarianism from Stalin, through Hitler, to Pol Pot. A Revolution which caused

intense strife and civil war is not a subject for celebration. The con-
demnatory, as well as the celebratory, legend is therefore very much
alive.

Historians of the Revolution can seldom escape the political
preoccupations of their own day, preoccupations which tend to
shape their interpretation of the past. Even the giants of Revolutionary scholarship were not above using history in an instrumental
fashion. Alphonse Aulard (1849–1928), the first holder of the pres-
tigious Professorship of the History of the Revolution at the Sor-
bonne, established in 1891, produced history designed to legitimise
the Third Republic and support radical resistance to royalism and
clericalism. Albert Mathiez (1874–1932) was a Marxist who wrote
historical works during the First World War partly intended to intensify the French war effort and seek outright military victory over
Germany. Georges Lefebvre (1874–1959), who also wrote from a
Marxist standpoint, published his *The Coming of the French Revolution
(Quatre-vingt-neuf)* in 1939 for the 150th anniversary in order to encourage Frenchmen to unite in defence of liberty and equality
against the threat from the Third Reich abroad and quasi-fascist
French political parties at home. Since the death of Lefebvre, the
Marxist dominance of Revolutionary studies has been loosened,
despite the voluminous writings of Albert Soboul (1914–82),
Lefebvre's most eminent pupil. Attacks on the Marxist 'Great
Tradition' have come from French revisionist historians and English
and American scholars. Such developments, however, have not
produced any general consensus on the Revolution, as historians
remain entrenched in their Marxist and revisionist camps, with historical scholarship still linked to political attitudes.

It remains difficult to strike a balance between the positive and
negative effects of the Revolution. Clearly, the Revolution achieved
much that was positive. The work of the National (Constituent) Assembly was remarkable, transforming all France's major institutions
and creating a new society and new approaches to the scope of political action, even if it did condone violence and make a hash of the
religious settlement. In his didactic and propagandistic *Reflections on
the Revolution in France* (1790), Edmund Burke brilliantly argued that
it was not possible to destroy a country's institutions and construct
a new society from a blank sheet (**260**, ch. 6). But the National
Assembly proved him wrong, even if the ultimate cost was enormous. A chaotic inheritance of privileges, prejudices and provincial
rights was swept away in favour of a new, rationalistic national
order, dedicated to the principle that power be entrusted only to

those who had been chosen by their fellow citizens, whether they were judges, bishops or National Guard officers. A belief in fundamental natural rights led to religious toleration, civil and political rights for Protestants and Jews, freedom of the press, equality before the law and trial by jury. The declaration of the Rights of Man in August 1789 contained a programme that was largely implemented over the next two years. The administrative reorganisation into departments, clearing away the jumble of jurisdictions which had developed piecemeal over centuries, still survives.

France was therefore transformed in ways which most of its educated citizens, at least, regarded as being for the better. And the Revolution was initially and primarily a movement of the educated and of intellectuals. The new institutions took root and survived all the vicissitudes of nineteenth-century France, even if in the short run the transformation was to tear the country apart and lead to foreign war, civil war and Terror, as well as the temporary suspension of most of the 'fundamental natural rights'. Although the declaration of war in 1792 was a disastrous error, the Convention deserves some credit for coping with its consequences and constructing the military and administrative machine which defeated the counter-revolution at home, split the coalition of France's enemies and enabled subsequent French expansion into Europe; although again at terrible cost.

In some other ways the Revolution did not change France all that much, with the important exception of the sweeping away of seigneurialism, or what the Revolutionaries preferred to call 'feudalism'. The nobility were far from being destroyed, for only 1,158 out of 400,000 or so were executed, while 16,431 emigrated, many only temporarily. The majority of noble families remained relatively unaffected materially by the Revolution and Terror, although the loss of seigneurial rights meant that their status in society was never the same again (**244**; **258**, ch. 8). It is true that the noble share of land-ownership fell, but the transfer of property during the Revolution was not quite so drastic as one might expect. Those who purchased the *biens nationaux* and confiscated property of *suspects* and *émigrés* usually already possessed land; more often than not they were the urban bourgeoisie, although many peasants acquired land during the late 1790s and subsequent decades (**29**; **35**; **258**, ch. 5). Among those who benefited the most were the financiers, speculators and bureaucrats who handled the finances of the Republic (and later the Empire). There was remarkable continuity between the financiers of the *ancien régime*, the Revolution, the Empire and the post-1815

Restoration. Great fortunes, founded on shady speculation by officials and administrators in the 1790s, not only enriched many bourgeois, but also some of the nobility whom the Revolution had attempted to decimate (**251**). The Church also survived, despite losing nearly half the parish clergy from death and emigration and suffering untold damage to buildings and property. Having benefited from a considerable religious revival after Thermidor, the Roman Catholic Church became the religion of 'the majority of Frenchmen' by the 1801 Concordat between Napoleon and the Papacy. Yet neither under the Empire nor the Bourbon restoration did the Church regain the land, wealth, personnel, prestige and respect it had enjoyed under the *ancien régime*.

Divine-Right monarchy had also gone for good. So had the old aristocratic and hierarchical society, for the restorations under Napoleon and Louis XVIII were only partial. After 1795 France possessed a more open and fluid society where careers were accessible to talent and ownership of property was more widely diffused. The power of the press and public opinion could never be completely stifled, even by Napoleon. On the other hand the violence of the Revolution, especially the Terror of the Year II and the White Terror of the Year III, left France badly divided and difficult to govern. The instability of French administrations in the nineteenth and early twentieth centuries owes a good deal to the antagonisms and tensions created both by the Revolution itself and by the myths which grew up about it after Thermidor*.

The Jacobin Republic of 1792–94 provided, for those willing to ignore the violence, a model of a militant minority determined to implement the ideal of the total sovereignty of the people, a model which was to inspire popular agitation – liberal, nationalist and socialist – both in France and abroad, even though there could never be agreement on just what the 'sovereignty of the people' implied in practice. It also demonstrated how a revolution can go wrong when the sovereignty of the people comes to mean the government telling people what they ought to want, rather than what they actually did want. In the Thermidorian period, Francois-Nöel Babeuf developed primitive socialist theories whose egalitarianism was to link Jacobinism with nineteenth-century socialism. The 'constitutional' Revolution of 1789–91 created a restricted, property-owning political democracy which helped inspire moderate middle-class European liberalism during the following century, especially when such liberals forgot about the howling mobs in the public galleries of the Assembly. The example of the *sans culottes* and the Revolutionary insurrections inspired oppressed peoples to seek their own versions of direct democracy and popular sovereignty.

At the same time it prompted rulers, nobles and clergy to unite in defence of the *status quo ante*. Reforming monarchs and enlightened despots retreated into conservatism, or rather developed it as a doctrine for the first time, fearing that the French epidemic would prove contagious. Whatever the strength of the forces of reaction in both France and Europe after the end of the Revolutionary and Napoleonic Wars in 1815, there was much that could never be erased. Warfare itself was put on a new footing; the intricate manoeuvring of many eighteenth-century armies had passed away, while armies themselves were larger and suffered much greater casualties. The Revolutionaries had taken the unprecedented step of arming the people.

While the sources of liberal democracy may be sought in the English Revolution of the 1640s and 1688, as well as the American Revolution of 1776–83, the French Revolution in its 1789–92 stage made a further major contribution. The increased power of wealth, as opposed to birth, in industrial society can at least partly be traced back to 1789 (**253**). And the concept of 'revolution' itself, in its modern sense, was also a product of the French Revolution (**265**, ch. 17).

There are those who now argue that the Revolution was not worth the costs involved and that, overall, it was a tragedy of gigantic proportions (**252; 267**). The first figure to list in the debit column is the two million dead in war and civil war between 1792 and 1815, more, in proportion to population, than in the First World War. Millions more had their lives ruined. Paper money, mass mobilisation and requisitioning during the Terror ruined an economy already shaken by civil and foreign war. To cope with rampant inflation, partly caused by their unrestrained issue of paper money, Revolutionary governments introduced price and wage controls which drove goods off the market, obliged the authorities to requisition food from recalcitrant peasants by force of arms, made bread even scarcer and helped to provoke a rebellion in the Vendée region whose repression involved virtual genocide. Issues of civic loyalty and treason in wartime inflicted yet more suffering on the French people, as small-scale massacres were transformed into official Terror.

Between 1793 and 1794 some 30,000 were killed in the 'official' Terror alone and tens of thousands imprisoned without trial in over-crowded, stinking gaols. Jean-Baptiste Carrier, the *représentant*\* in the rebellious west, turned the Loire into a 'national bathtub', drowning prisoners in batches of hundreds at Nantes and reporting to Paris: 'We shall turn France into a cemetery rather than fail in her regeneration'. Even though the Terror did not last long, its legacy was the reintroduction of the spirit of religious warfare to a country and a continent which had virtually forgotten it. Both politics and war became black-and-white struggles between good and evil, with compromise or negotiation ruled out of court.

The Revolutionaries first introduced and then restricted freedom of the individual, of the press and of association; but they never limited the power of the state or its police. When the Bastille was taken on 14 July 1789 it was found to contain only seven prisoners; five years later the gaols of the Republic bulged with over 400,000 inmates. No sooner was the ink dry on the Declaration of the Rights of Man than the National Assembly set up committees to report on potential counter-revolutionary plots, to open mail, to arrest suspects without warrant and detain them without due process of law. Determined to re-shape humanity, the Revolutionaries re-cast France into new administrative units, replaced local laws by national ones, and attempted to replace local speech and currencies with national means of exchange – French and the *franc*. The metric system, in itself eminently sensible and eventually copied through the world, formed the basis of new national measurements, designed to replace the jungle of weights and measures embedded for centuries in local communities. Although Revolutionary leaders aspired to extend popular primary education, little was done about it, and in 1815 about 5 per cent fewer people could read or sign their names than in 1789.

Not only did the Revolution devour many of its children, as well as many of other people's, but it also destroyed much of France's cultural heritage. The *ancien régime*\* and its associations had to be eradicated. Noble and monastic libraries were pillaged, confiscated or destroyed. Charters, parchments, manuscripts, books – all were seen as remnants of 'feudal oppression' and burned in public ceremonies. Inscriptions, coats of arms, sculptures that recalled 'superstition' (that is, Christianity) or the 'tyrannical past' were removed, defaced or hammered out in an orgy of destruction. The 231 statues of Strasbourg Cathedral were shattered; so were the 28 thirteenth-century statues of Biblical royalty on the façade of Notre Dame – decapitated on 23 October 1793 under the impression that they represented Kings of France. Rouen Cathedral became blackened from use as a gunpowder factory. Chartres Cathedral escaped 'patriotic demolition' only because the contractors judged it would create too much dangeous debris in the narrow streets. But the abbey of Saint-Denis just outside Paris, the traditional burying-place of French monarchs, had its roof stripped, its stained glass shattered and the tombs of 51 Kings and Queens of France desecrated by order of the Convention. Churches, abbeys and castles were demolished by the score. Spires and bell-towers were razed; so were royal *châteaux* and palaces. This destruction marked popular revenge for the repression and humiliation that so many had suffered at the hands of the nobility and clergy before 1789, and to lament such large-scale vandalism is to run the risk of playing down the repressive and unjust aspects of seigneurialism.

No serious historian, however, denies that France's economy suffered severe damage during the Revolution. Population growth slowed after 1789, with France having more spinsters and widows than England because of war deaths. The sale of between 15 and 20 per cent of French land belonging to the Church, *émigrés* and *suspects\** more than doubled the number of landowners, but failed to stimulate agricultural productivity. Many of the new owners lacked capital and experience of farming, while agriculture itself was badly affected by labour shortages, fixed prices and depreciating *assignats\**. Grain production in 1815 was no higher than in 1789, while there were fewer sheep, cows and horses. During the same period, England's agrarian productivity rose rapidly. So did her industrial lead, as the French concentrated overwhelmingly on the production of war materials. Before 1789, according to François Crouzet, French industry had been able to match that of England. But this was no longer the case during and after the Revolution. Industry was drained of its competitiveness by a quarter-century of revolution and war, being able to survive only under cover of protective tariffs.

Trade also suffered. The war meant maritime blockade, the decline of shipping and the decay of great ports like Nantes, Bordeaux and Marseille. France's road network fell to pieces from neglect and shortage of funds; bridges and tunnels collapsed. Freedom of trade was soon negated by a mass of regulations and restrictions. Bad for business, the Revolutionary years were good only for war contractors, speculators, crooks and smugglers. Nor were Revolutionary governments ever able to solve the financial crisis which had brought down the royal administration. Indeed, the deficit continued to increase and in 1797 the French nation declared itself bankrupt. Whether military glory and the expansion of the French empire under Napoleon were sufficient compensation for so much damage and so many ruined lives seems arguable at the very least.

Yet there are historians on the Left who still emphasise how the peasants, who accounted for 70 per cent of the population in 1789, gained three major benefits which they were to guard jealously over the subsequent century: the end of seigneurialism, eventual access to more land, and a more impartial system of justice (**258**, ch. 8). Others point to the fact that the concept of revolution cannot be exorcised or deemed increasingly irrelevant to the modern world, in which gross inequalities and pervasive social injustice produce revolutionary situations. Nor are they happy with revisionist interpretations which play down social and economic causes of the Revolution in favour of political and ideological factors.

While such arguments retain their force, they tend to neglect the experiences of people at the time in favour of posterity, and there seems little doubt that the celebratory tradition of Revolutionary scholarship cannot survive without serious modification. Historians of the counter-revolution have drawn upon a wide range of local studies to demonstrate that most French people were opposed to what was being done in Paris from 1790 onwards. They had revolted against centralisation and the attempt to increase royal state power, but found that Revolutionary centralising policies vastly enhanced the power of the state. While many peasants made material gains, there were many others who proved unwilling to accept either the Civil Constitution of the Clergy or military conscription. If there was a widespread genuinely popular movement during the Revolution, it was not that of the militant *sans culottes*; rather the real popular movement was the counter-revolution, not as expressed in armed risings, which were largely confined to the west and south-east, but in the sense that most ordinary people resented what had happened to them since 1789 and, when circumstances permitted, did not hesitate to take action against local Jacobins and government officials. They certainly did not wish to restore the Bourbons or the *ancien régime*, but wanted simply to be left alone with whatever gains they had made in 1789. What happened after 1790 tended to be resented. Indeed, only the fact that the Revolution was resented by so many of those who had to endure it can explain the vigour and extent of the resistance to successive Revolutionary governments. And the extent of this resistance means that the Revolution was, in the end, a tragedy, and one to be analysed and debated rather than simply celebrated. It may be going too far to argue that the Revolution was a repulsively violent interlude in an otherwise vigorously maturing society (**264**). Yet no revolution has been, or ever could be, 'one and indivisible'. Very few modern historians would unreservedly endorse the view of Charles James Fox that the Revolution was 'the greatest event in human history and the best'. Revolutions generate hope, energy and Utopian aspirations. At the same time they all too often produce mass bloodshed and a tendency to focus on what men ought to be rather than what they actually are. It was Saint-Just who, defending the excesses of the Terror of 1793–94, defined 'humanity' as 'the extermination of one's enemies'.

When Marie Antoinette went to the scaffold, her once-beautiful hands tied behind her, she accidentally trod on the foot of her executioner and immediately apologised. For the next 180 years the French nation found it impossible to find a universally acceptable substitute for her late husband: 'Louis, by the Grace of God, King of France and of Navarre'. François Furet's 1978 essay 'The French Revolution is over' proved misguided (**23**). The bicentenary celebrations and debates showed that the French people are still deeply divided over their 'indigestible revolution' (**270**). It will continue to be so for the foreseeable future, certainly until all those who supported the Popular Front in the late 1930s and the Resistance during the war, as well as those who thought (or even said) 'Better Hitler than Blum' and supported the Vichy regime in collaborating with the Nazi occupation, have been long in their graves.

# Part Five:   Documents

Translations are by the author unless otherwise indicated.

**document 1**

## The effects of rural poverty in 1789

*The following extracts from four of the 25,000 'cahiers de doléances' illustrate the tensions created at the bottom of rural society by the economic crisis of the late 1780s and help to explain the peasant risings and the 'Great Fear'.*

(a)   *Rural degeneracy in Pleurs, Bailliage de Sézanne*

Afflicted by so many misfortunes and suffering from poverty, the people of the countryside have become listless; they have fallen into a state of numbness, a kind of apathy, which is the most dangerous of all complaints and the most disastrous for the prosperity of a country. The population is suffering. They are afraid to get married, for marriage only holds the prospect of further hardships; they would immediately be taxed, asked for road services or charges (*corvées*), for labour services and contributions of all kinds. They fear a situation where their family would be a burden on them, since they can only anticipate their children being poor and wretched.

Oh petty tyrants placed at the heart of the provinces to hold sway over their destinies! Oh proprietors of seigneurial estates who demand the most crippling and servile exactions! Oh rich citizens who own property for the moment! Be so good as to leave for a time your palaces and châteaux, leave your towns where you have created new problems, where you are offered with both hands every indulgence and luxury which artisans can invent to stimulate your blunted senses, your satiated spirits; be so good as to glance at those unfortunate men whose muscles are only occupied in working for you! What do you see in our villages, in our fields? A few enfeebled men, whose pale faces are withered by poverty and shame, their wives lamenting their fecundity, each child wearing rags.

Among them, however, you will find several who are happy; these seem to be men of a different kind; they are in fact privileged men like you, nourished on the food of the people; they live amid abundance and each day is pure and serene for them. Such a striking comparison has served to deepen the misery of the labourer, if he is at all sensitive.

(b)   *Robbery and pillage in Lugny-Champagne, Bailliage de Bourges*
The inhabitants of the parish of Lugny-Champagne are complaining that at the beginning of the harvest time there arrived in the district a huge number of male and female gleaners from other areas, who flooded into fields that were still covered with sheaves and spread themselves everywhere, even among the fields not yet harvested; the men in charge of the fields could not get them out; not only did they glean among the sheaves, but they seized fistsful of grain from the sheaves themselves; if the farmer tried to say anything, they poured abuse on him; they even chased away the very poor of the village. To guard against such inconvenience, the inhabitants want no itinerants to be allowed to glean, because young men and women are then unwilling to do the work, even at high wages; and as for those who are not travellers, like widows, poor women and their children, they must only be permitted to glean if they have a certificate of good character signed by their priest.

(c)   *Vagabonds in Marsainvilliers and Chaon, Bailliage d'Orléans*
It is not possible for the inhabitants of Marsainvilliers to arrest the beggars; that would be to expose them to frequent attack, even to gunfire. The inhabitants of Chaon are angry when they see so many wretches cast themselves on public charity and thus take the money due to the genuine poor; often they enrich themselves, under the cloak of poverty, and having thus spent their lives. . . die opulent and leave small fortunes to the children they have brought up in idleness and mendacity.

French texts in P. Goubert and M. Denis, eds, *1789 Les Français ont la parole: cahiers des États Généraux*, Paris, Julliard, 1964.

**document 2**
## The overthrow of feudalism

*This complaint to the National Assembly on 20 August 1789 shows how, in many parts of the country, peasants took violent action against the feudal régime.*

... On 29 July 1789, a group of brigands from elsewhere, together with my vassals and those of Virgni, the next parish to mine, two hundred in all, came to my *château* at Sassy, parish of Saint Christopher, near Argentan, and, after breaking the locks on the cupboards containing my title deeds, they seized the registers which could be so necessary to me and took them away, or burned them in the woods near my *château*; my guard was unable to offer any resistance, being the only warden in this area, where I myself do not reside. These wretched people had the tocsin rung in neighbouring parishes in order to swell their numbers. I am all the more sad about this loss because I have never let my vassals feel the odious weight of ancient feudalism, of which I am sure they could be redeemed in present circumstances; but who will ever be able to certify and prove the damage that they have inflicted on my property? I appeal to your discretion to bring in some law whereby the National Assembly can reimburse me for my loss, above all for the use of common land, as useful to my parishioners as to my own estate, whose title deeds they burned. I will not take steps against those whom I know to have been with the brigands who, not content with burning my papers, have killed all my pigeons. But I expect full justice in the spirit of equity which guides you, and which gives me the greatest confidence.

COMTE DE GERMINY

P. Sagnac and P. Caron, *Les Comités de droits féodaux et législation et l'abolition du régime seigneurial 1789–1793*, Paris, 1907, p. 158.

## document 3
## The declaration of the rights of man and the citizen, 1789

*The declaration was very much the charter of the 'patriot' educated middle classes who led the Revolution.*

The representatives of the French people, sitting in the National Assembly considering that ignorance of, neglect of, and contempt for the rights of man are the sole causes of public misfortune and the corruption of governments, have resolved to set out in a solemn declaration the natural, inalienable and sacred rights of man, in order that this declaration, constantly before all members of the civic body, will constantly remind them of their rights and duties, in order that acts of legislative and executive power can be frequently compared with the purpose of every political institution, thus making them more respected; in order that the demands of the citizens, henceforth founded on simple and irrefutable principles, will always tend towards the maintenance of the constitution and the happiness of everyone.

Consequently the National Assembly recognises and declares, in the presence of, and under the auspices of, the Supreme Being, the following rights of man and of the citizen:

i   Men are born and remain free and equal in rights. Social distinctions can only be founded on communal utility.

ii   The purpose of all political associations is the preservation of the natural and imprescriptible rights of man. These rights are liberty, property, security and resistance to oppression.

iii   The principle of all sovereignty emanates essentially from the nation. No group of men, no individual, can exercise any authority which does not specifically emanate from it.

iv   Liberty consists in being able to do whatever does not harm others. Hence the exercise of the natural rights of every man is limited only by the need for other members of society to exercise the same rights. These limits can only be determined by the law.

v   The law only has the right to prohibit actions harmful to society. What is not prohibited by law cannot be forbidden, and nobody can be forced to do what the law does not require.

vi   The law is the expression of the general will. All citizens have the right to take part personally, or through their representatives, in the making of the law. It should be the same for everyone, whether it protects or punishes. All citizens, being equal in the eyes of the law, are equally admissible to all honours, offices and public employment, according to their capacity and without any distinction other than those of their integrity and talents.

vii   A man can only be accused, arrested or detained in cases determined by law, and according to the procedure it requires. Those who solicit, encourage, execute, or cause to be executed, arbitrary orders must be punished, but every citizen called upon or arrested in the name of the law must obey instantly; resistance renders him culpable.

viii   The law must only require punishments that are strictly and evidently necessary, and a person can only be punished according to an established law passed before the offence and legally applied.

ix Every man being presumed innocent until he has been declared guilty, if it is necessary to arrest him, all severity beyond what is necessary to secure his arrest shall be severely punished by law.

x No man ought to be uneasy about his opinions, even his religious beliefs, provided that their manifestation does not interfere with the public order established by the law.

xi The free communication of thought and opinion is one of the most precious rights of man: every citizen can therefore talk, write and publish freely, except that he is responsible for abuses of this liberty in cases determined by the law.

xii The guaranteeing of the rights of man and the citizen requires a public force: this force is therefore established for everybody's advantage and not for the particular benefit of the persons who are entrusted with it.

xiii A common contribution is necessary for the maintenance of the public force and for administrative expenses; it must be equally apportioned between all citizens, according to their means.

xiv All citizens have the right, personally or by means of their representatives, to have demonstrated to them the necessity of public taxes, so that they can consent freely to them, can check how they are used, and can determine the shares to be paid, their assessment, collection and duration.

xv The community has the right to hold accountable every public official in its administration.

xvi Every society which has no assured guarantee of rights, nor a separation of powers, does not possess a constitution.

xvii Property being a sacred and inviolable right, nobody can be deprived of it, except when the public interest, legally defined, evidently requires it, and then on condition there is just compensation in advance.

French text in J. M. Thompson, *French Revolution Documents 1789–94*, Blackwell 1933, pp. 109–11.

**document 4**

# The 'problème des subsistances', 1789

*Bailly, a distinguished mathematician and astronomer, was one of the popular heroes of 1789. The first president of the National Assembly, he became Mayor of Paris on 15 July. His diary reveals the enormity of the problem of supplying the Paris market with food and the accepted link between bread and insurrection.*

26 August: I have already demanded that attention be devoted to the provisioning of Paris with grain. I returned today to the Assembly, and I asked that attention be given to providing the capital with food for the early winter months, observing that we can only obtain it from foreign sources. I saw that the grain bought by the government is running out. I thought that in a disastrous period, at the time of a good harvest, but one which will start being consumed two or three months earlier than usual, it was necessary to have a stockpile of food in reserve, to prevent any cause for, or pretext for, an insurrection and that such a stockpile could only be obtained abroad. . . The cartloads of flour in our convoys are not only pillaged on the way by mobs, but are also pillaged in Paris by bakers who wait for them in the *faubourgs*. . . such disorder creates two serious problems: the first is that the distribution of flour is unequal: one baker has too much, another not enough; the second is that the Paris Market is poorly stocked, which disturbs public opinion.

*Mémoires de Bailly*, Paris, 1821–22, ii, 304–5.

**document 5**

# The clerical oath, 27 November 1790

The National Assembly . . . decrees as follows:
  i The bishops, former archbishops, and curés still in office, will be required, if they have not already done so, to take the oath . . . they will swear . . . carefully to look after the faithful of the diocese, or of the parish with which they have been entrusted; to be faithful to the nation, to the law and to the king, and to preserve with all their power the constitution which has been decreed by the National Assembly and accepted by the king . . . .

viii We will pursue, as violators of public order, and punish according to the rigours of the law, all ecclesiastical and lay persons who combine together in order to refuse to obey the decrees of the National Assembly, accepted and sanctioned by the king, or who try to form or arouse opposition to their execution.

French text Thompson, *op. cit.*, pp. 80–2.

## The influence of the Jacobin Club, 1791 document 6

*From May 1789 'patriots' came together to discuss political problems. This was the origin of the political clubs, including the Breton Club. After October 1789 it met in the old Jacobin monastery in the Rue St Honoré as the Société des Amis de la Constitution', now open to the middle classes generally as well as deputies. It soon became known as the Jacobin Club and corresponded with clubs founded in the principal provincial towns. This report is from Camille Desmoulins' brilliant weekly paper.*

In the propagation of patriotism, that is to say of philanthropy, this new religion which is bound to conquer the universe, the club or church of the Jacobins seems destined for the same primacy as that of the church of Rome in the propagation of Christianity. Already all the clubs and assemblies and churches of patriots, which are being formed everywhere, demand correspondence with it and write to it as a sign of fraternity. . . . The Jacobin Society is truly the committee of inquiry of the nation, less dangerous to good citizens than that of the National Assembly, because the denunciations, the deliberations are public there; much more formidable to bad citizens, because it covers by its correspondence with affiliated societies all the nooks and crannies of the 83 *départements*. Not only is it the great investigator which terrifies the aristocrats; it is also the great investigator which redresses all abuses and comes to the aid of all citizens. It seems that in reality the club acts as a public ministry alongside the National Assembly. They come from everywhere to place the grievances of the oppressed at its feet, before taking their complaints to the worthy Assembly. In the assembly hall of the Jacobins there is an increasing flow of deputations, missions of congratulation, those seeking close relations with the club, those seeking to promote vigilance, or those seeking the redress of injustices.

*Les Révolutions de France et de Brabant,* 14 February 1791.

**document 7**
# The overthrow of the monarchy: 10 August 1792

*This letter, sent by a National Guard to a friend in Rennes, describes the events of 10 August and the following days. Despite being from the point of view of a participant, it keeps a reasonably objective tone.*

Paris – 11 August 1792 – Year 4 of Liberty
We are all tired out, doubtless less from spending two nights under arms than from heartache. Men's spirits were stirred after the unfortunate decree which whitewashed Lafayette. Nevertheless, we had a quiet enough evening; a group of *fédérés* from Marseille gaily chanted patriotic songs in the Beaucaire café, the refreshment room of the National Assembly. It was rumoured 'Tonight the tocsin will ring, the alarm drum will be beaten. All the *faubourgs* will burst into insurrection, supported by 6,000 *fédérés*.' At 11 o'clock we go home, at the same instant as the drums call us back to arms. We speed from our quarters and our battalion, headed by two pieces of artillery, marches to the palace. Hardly have we reached the garden of the Tuileries than we hear the alarm cannon. The alarm drum resounds through all the streets of Paris. People run for arms from all over the place. Soon the public squares, the new bridge, the main thoroughfares, are covered with troops. The National Assembly, which had finished its debate early, was recalled to its duties. It only knew of some of the preparations which had been made for the *Journée* of 10 August. First the commandant of the palace wishes to hold the mayor a hostage there, then he sends him to the mayor's office. The people fear a display of his talents! In the general council of the Commune it is decreed that, according to the wishes of the forty-eight sections, it is no longer necessary to recognise the constituted authorities if dethronement is not immediately announced and new municipal bodies, keeping Pétion and Manuel at their head, entrusted with popular authority. However, the *faubourgs* organised themselves into an army and placed in their centre Bretons, Marseillais and Bordelais, and all the other *fédérés*. More than 20,000 men march across Paris, bristling with pikes and bayonets. Santerre had been obliged to take command of them. The National Assembly are told that the army has broken into the palace. All hearts are frozen. Discussion is provoked again by the question of the safety of the king, when it is learned that Louis XVI seeks refuge in the bosom of the Assembly.
Forty-eight members are sent to the palace. The royal family

places itself in the middle of the deputation. The people fling bitter reproaches at the king and accuse him of being the author of his troubles. Hardly was the king safe than the noise of cannon-fire increased. The Breton *fédérés* beat a tattoo. Some officers suggested retreat to the commander of the Swiss guards. But he seemed prepared and soon, by a clever tactic, captured the artillery which the National Guard held in the courtyard. These guns, now turned on the people, fire and strike them down. But soon the conflict is intensified everywhere. The Swiss, surrounded, overpowered, stricken, then run out of ammunition. They plead for mercy, but it is impossible to calm the people, furious at Helvetian treachery.

The Swiss were cut to pieces. Some were killed in the state-rooms, others in the garden. Many died on the Champs-Élysées. Heavens! That Liberty should cost Frenchmen blood and tears! How many victims there were among both the People and the National Guard! The total number of dead could run to 2,000. All the Swiss who had been taken prisoner were escorted to the Place de Grève. There they had their brains blown out. They were traitors sacrificed to vengeance. What vengeance! I shivered to the roots of my being. At least 47 heads were cut off. The Grève was littered with corpses, and heads were paraded on the ends of several pikes. The first heads to be severed were those of seven *chevaliers du poignard*, slain at eight o'clock in the morning on the Place Vendôme. Many Marseillais perished in the *journée* of 10 August. Their second-in-command was killed, so was the commander of the Bretons.

The bronze statues in the Place Royale, Place Vendôme, Place Louis XIV, Place Louis XV, are thrown to the ground. The Swiss are pursued everywhere. The National Assembly, the department and the municipality are in permanent session. . . . People are still far from calm and it will be difficult to re-establish order. However, we see peace starting to reappear. The king and his family have passed the night in the porter's lodging of the National Assembly.

Tonight the National Assembly has decreed [the creation of] the National Convention. The electors are gathered in primary assemblies to select deputies. They only need to be twenty-five years old and have a residence qualification. It appears that the *coup* of 10 August has forestalled one by the aristocracy. One realizes now that the Swiss are the victims of their credulity, that they hoped for support, but that the rich men who should have fought with them dared not put in an appearance. We have been told that there are 8,000 royalist grenadiers in Paris. These 8,000 citizens seem to have stayed at home. Only one equestrian statue has been preserved in the capital: that of Henri IV.

MS letter in John Rylands Library, University of Manchester.

**document 8**

## La Vendée, 1793

*This report by two refugees from Saint-Pierre-de-Chemillé describes a typical band of Vendéan rebels.*

Wednesday, 13 March, about 5 in the afternoon, a large number of men in a band, armed with guns, hooks, forks, scythes and so on, all wearing white cockades and decorated with small, square, cloth medallions, on which are embroidered different shapes, such as crosses, little hearts pierced with pikes, and other signs of that kind, appeared in the township of Saint-Pierre. All these fellows shouted 'Long live the King and our Good Priests! We want our king, our priests and the old régime!' And they wanted to kill off all the patriots, especially us two witnesses. All that band, which was terrifyingly large, hurled itself at the Patriots, who had gathered to resist their attempt. They killed many, made many others prisoner, and scattered the rest.

Archives départementales, Maine-et-Loire, K1018.

**document 9**

## *Levée en masse:* 23 August 1793

*This decree marks the appearance of total war.*

i From this time, until the enemies of France have been expelled from the territory of the Republic, all Frenchmen are in a state of permanent requisition for the army. The young men will go to fight; married men will forge arms and transport food and supplies; women will make tents and uniforms and work in hospitals; children will find old rags for bandages; old men will appear in public places to excite the courage of warriors, the hatred of kings, and the unity of the Republic.

ii Public buildings will be converted into barracks, public

squares into armament workshops, the soil of cellars will be washed to extract saltpetre.

iii Rifles will be confined exclusively to those who march to fight the enemy; military service in the interior will be performed with sporting guns and side-arms.

iv Riding horses will be requisitioned for the cavalry corps; draught horses, other than those used in agriculture, will pull artillery and stores.

v The Committee of Public Safety is charged with the taking of all measures to establish, without delay, an extraordinary factory for arms of all kinds, to cater for the determination and energy of the French people; it is consequently authorised to form as many establishments, factories, workshops and mills as are necessary to carry out the work, as well as requiring, for this purpose, throughout the Republic, craftsmen and workers who can contribute to its success; for this object there is a sum of 30 millions at the disposal of the ministry of war . . .

French text in Thompson, *op. cit.*, pp. 255–6.

## What is a *sans culotte*? document 10

*This document represents the* sans culottes' *view of themselves.* L'Ami des Lois *was a fashionable comedy of 1793,* Chaste Susanne *a light operetta;* Gorsas *was a Girondin journalist;* La Chronique *and* Patriot Francais *were Girondin newspapers.*

A *sans culotte*, you rogues? He is someone who always goes about on foot, who has not got the millions you would all like to have, who has no châteaux, no valets to wait on him, and who lives simply with his wife and children, if he has any, on the fourth or fifth storey. He is useful because he knows how to till a field, to forge iron, to use a saw, to roof a house, to make shoes, and to spill his blood to the last drop for the safety of the Republic. And because he is a worker, you are sure not to meet his person in the Café de Chartres, or in the gaming houses where others plot and wager, nor in the National Theatre, where *L'Ami des Lois* is performed, nor in the Vaudeville Theatre at a performance of *Chaste Susanne*, nor in the literary clubs where for two sous, which are so precious to him, you are offered Gorsas's muck, with the *Chronique* and *the Patriot Français*.

In the evening he goes to the assembly of his Section, not powdered and perfumed and nattily booted, in the hope of being noticed by the citizenesses in the galleries, but ready to support sound proposals with all his might and ready to pulverise those which come from the despised faction of politicians.

Finally, a *sans culotte* always has his sabre well-sharpened, ready to cut off the ears of all opponents of the Revolution; sometimes he carries his pike about with him; but as soon as the drum beats you see him leave for the Vendée, for the Army of the Alps, or for the Army of the North.

Archives Nationales, F7 4775/48, dossier Vinternier.

## document 11
## A *sans culotte* definition of a *feuillant* (an aristocrat and a moderate)

*This document shows who the* sans culottes *regarded as enemies of the people. Note the political definition of 'aristocrat'.*

The aristocrat is a man who, because of his scorn or indifference, has not been entered on the register of National Guards and who has not taken the civic oath. . . . He is a man who, by his conduct, his activities, his speeches and his writings, as well as by his connections, has given proof that he bitterly regrets the passing of the *ancien régime* and despises every aspect of the Revolution. He is a man whose conduct suggests that he would send cash to the *émigrés* or join the enemy army, if only he had the means to do the one and the opportunity to do the other. He is a man who has always despaired of the triumph of the Revolution, who has spread bad news which is obviously false. He is a man who by inefficient management has left land uncultivated, without letting any to farmers or selling any at a fair price. He is a man who has not purchased any national wealth (*biens nationaux*) whilst having both the resources and the opportunity. Above all, he is a man who declared that he would not buy them and advised others not to perform this act of civic duty. He is a man who, though he has the resources and the opportunity, has not provided work for journeymen and workmen at a wage level above that of the price of basic necessities. He is a man who has not subscribed to the fund for the Volunteers, and certainly has not given as much as he could. He is a man who, because of aristocratic pride, does not visit the civil clergy, and what is more advised others not to do so. He is a man who has done nothing to ameliorate the lives of the poor and who does not wear a cockade of three inches circumference; a man who has bought clothes other than national dress and who takes no pride in the title and clothing of a *sans culotte*. The true language of the Republic assures you that this definition is just and that the true patriot has done quite the opposite for the well-being of the Republic.

Archives Nationales, D xl 23, d, 77, p. 35, May 1793.

**document 12**

## The *sans culotte* programme

*The following address, sent to the Convention by the* Section des Sans Culottes *on 2 September 1793, summarises the social and economic aims of the more extreme* sans culottes *and marks the nearest they came to a concrete programme of social equality.*

Mandatories of the People – Just how long are you going to tolerate royalism, ambition, egotism, intrigue and avarice, each of them linked to fanaticism, and opening our frontiers to tyranny, whilst spreading devastation and death everywhere? How long are you going to suffer food-hoarders spreading famine throughout the Republic in the detestable hope that patriots will cut each other's throats and the throne will be restored over our bloody corpses, with the help of foreign despots? You must hurry for there is no time to lose . . . the whole universe is watching you: humanity reproaches you for the troubles which are devastating the French Republic. Posterity will damn your names in future if you do not speedily find a remedy. . . . You must hurry, representatives of the people, to deprive all former nobles, priests, *parlementaires* and financiers of all administrative and judicial responsibility; also to fix the price of basic foodstuffs, raw materials, wages, and the profits of industry and commerce. You have both the justification and the power to do so. To speak plainly! To talk of aristocrats, royalists, moderates and counter-revolutionaries is to draw attention to property rights, held to be sacred and inviolable . . . no doubt; but do these rogues ignore the fact that property rights are confined to the extent of the satisfaction of physical needs? Don't they know that nobody has the right to do anything that will injure another person? What could be more harmful than the arbitrary power to increase the price of basic necessities to a level beyond the means of seven eighths of the citizens? ... Do they not realize that every individual in the Republic must employ his intelligence and the strength of his arms in the service of the Republic, and must spill his blood for her to the very last drop? In return, the Republic should guarantee to each citizen the means of obtaining sufficient basic necessities to stay alive.

Would you not agree that we have passed a harsh law against hoarders? Representatives of the people, do not let the law be abused. ... This law, which forces those with large stocks of foodstuffs to declare their hoard, tends to favour hoarders more than it wipes out hoarding; it puts all their stocks under the supervision of the nation, yet permits them to charge whatever price their greed dictates. Consequently, the general assembly of the *Section des Sans Culottes* considers it to be the duty of all citizens to propose measures which seem likely to bring about a return of abundance and public tranquillity. It therefore resolves to ask the Convention to decree the following:

1.  That former nobles will be barred from military careers and every kind of public office; that former *parlementaires,* priests and financiers will be deprived of all administrative and judicial duties.

2.  That the price of basic necessities be fixed at the levels of 1789–90, allowing for differences in quality.

3.  That the price of raw materials, level of wages and profits of industry and commerce also be fixed, so that the hard-working man, the cultivator and the trader will be able to procure basic necessities, and also those things which add to their enjoyment.

4.  That all those cultivators who, by some accident, have not been able to harvest their crop, be compensated from public funds.

5.  That each department be allowed sufficient public money to ensure that the price of basic foodstuffs will be the same for all citizens of the Republic.

6.  That the sums of money allowed to departments be used to eradicate variations in the price of foodstuffs and necessities and in the cost of transporting them to all parts of the Republic, so that each citizen is equal in these things.

7.  That existing leases be cancelled and rents fixed at the levels of 1789–90, as for foodstuffs.

8. That there be a fixed maximum on personal wealth.
9. That no single individual shall possess more than the declared maximum.
10. That nobody be able to lease more land than is necessary for a fixed number of ploughs.
11. That no citizen shall possess more than one workshop or retail shop.
12. That all who possess goods and land without legal title be recognised as proprietors.

The *Section des Sans Culottes* thinks that these measures will create abundance and tranquillity, and will, little by little, remove the gross inequalities of wealth and multiply the number of proprietors.

Bibliothèque Nationale, Lb/40 2140.

**document 13**

## The law of *suspects*, 1793

*This law, passed on 17 September, cast the net of suspicion very wide indeed and was partly a response to* sans culotte *demands.*

1. Immediately after the publication of this decree, all *suspects* found on the territory of the Republic and who are still at liberty will be arrested.
2. *Suspects* are (i) Those who, either by their conduct or their relationships, by their conversation or by their writing, are shown to be partisans of tyranny and federalism and enemies of liberty; (ii) Those who cannot justify, under the provisions of the law of 21 March last, their means of existence and the performance of their civic duties; (iii) Those who have been refused certificates of civic responsibility; (iv) Public officials suspended or deprived of their functions by the National Convention or its agents, and not since reinstated, especially those who have been, or ought to be, dismissed by the law of 12 August last; (v) Those former nobles, including husbands, wives, fathers, mothers, sons or daughters, brothers or sisters, and agents of *émigrés*, who have not constantly manifested their loyalty to the Revolution; (vi) Those who have emigrated during the interval between the 1 July 1789 and the publication of the law of 8 April 1792, although they may have returned to France during the period of delay fixed by the law or before.

The *comités de surveillance* established under the law of 21 March last, or those substituting for them, are empowered by the decrees of the representatives of the people to go to the armies and the departments, according to the particular decrees of the National Convention, and are charged with drawing up, in each local district, a list of *suspects*, of issuing arrest warrants against them, and of affixing seals to their private papers. The commanders of the public force, to whom these arrest warrants will be conveyed, must carry them out immediately, on pain of dismissal.

French text in Thompson, *op. cit.*, pp. 258–9.


**document 14**
## The blade of vengeance

*This petition to the Convention from the William Tell section of Paris, dated 12 November 1793, illustrates the endorsement of the Terror by the militant sans culottes.*

[The execution of Marie Antoinette and the Girondin deputies] furnished a terrible example to astonish the universe and strike fear amongst the most guilty. Bloodshed is necessary in order to punish those who might follow their example. Representatives of the people, it will take more than the deaths of a fistful of conspirators to destroy all the strands of the most abominable plot to hatch in human breasts; there must be a public sacrifice of traitors to heal the wounds of a country slaughtered by its disfigured children. The aristocracy has not given up its shadowy and sinister plotting. Murder and carnage are its favourite foods; the fall of 21 heads [on 16 and 31 October 1793], that of the slut Marie Antoinette and the dissolute inhabitants of the palace of hell, has highlighted aristocratic fury and revealed in a flash its intention of knocking over the column of liberty. There are other enemies no less dangerous: the evil public robbers and plunderers. Legislators! Do not spare those vampires who suck the blood of *La Patrie;* scrutinise carefully the scandalous fortunes which remain an insult to the poverty of the people, and only close the graveyards when our most evil internal enemies have been swallowed up. Representatives, the days of forgiveness are now past; the blade of vengeance should fall on all guilty heads; the people await drastic measures which will make sure that the guilty are not spared. Do not forget the sublime words of the prophet Marat: 'Sacrifice two hundred thousand heads and you will save a million'.

Archives Nationales, C280, pl. 769, p. 38.

## The armée révolutionnaire at Lyon

*On 12 October 1793 the Convention decreed the destruction of the rebel city of Lyon and the setting up of a memorial with the inscription 'Lyon made war on liberty, Lyon no longer exists'. The remaining buildings were to be called* Commune-Affranchie. *Ronsin's letter tells of the role of the armée révolutionnaire of Paris in the conquest of Lyon.*

The General-in-Chief of the Revolutionary Army, to his brothers and friends the Cordeliers. The Revolutionary Army on 5 Frimaire (25 November 1793) entered that guilty city, so wrongly called *Commune Affranchie.* Terror was painted on every brow; and the complete silence that I had taken care to impose on our brave soldiers, made their march even more menacing, more terrible; most of the shops were closed: some women stood alongside our route; one read in their eyes more indignation than fear. The men remained hidden in their dens from which they had sallied forth, during the siege, only to assassinate the true friends of liberty.

The guillotine and the firing squad did justice to more than four hundred rebels. But a new revolutionary commission has just been established, consisting of true *sans culottes*: my colleague Parein is its president, and in a few days the grape-shot, fired by our cannoneers, will have delivered to us, in one single moment, more than four thousand conspirators. It is time to cut down the procedure! Delay can awaken, I will not say courage, but the despair of traitors who are still hidden among the debris of that impious town. The Republic has need of a great example – the Rhône, reddened with blood, must carry to its banks and to the sea, the corpses of those cowards who murdered our brothers; and whilst the thunderbolt, which must exterminate them in an instant, will carry terror into the departments where the seed of rebellion was sown, it is necessary that the flames from their devastated dens proclaim far and wide the punishment that is destined for those who try to imitate them.

These measures are all the more urgent because, in that commune of one hundred and twenty thousand inhabitants, you would scarcely find, I shall not say fifteen hundred patriots, but fifteen hundred men who had not been accomplices of the rebellion; but thanks to the representatives of the people and to the Jacobins, sent into the commune, the vigilance of the constituted authorities everywhere pursues suspect persons and paralyses, as it were, with fear, the great number of those who secretly aspire only to plunge their knives into us. Already the cowards have assassinated one of our revolutionary soldiers during the night; decide, then, brothers and friends, if it is not time to use the most prompt and most terrible means of justice! This great event is being prepared, and we hope that, before the end of Frimaire, all the authors and accomplices of the rebellion will have paid for their crimes.

*Salut et fraternité.*                                                     RONSIN

*Les Révolutions de Paris*, no. 218, 18–27 Frimaire, Year II (8–17 Dec. 1793). Translation from J. Gilchrest and W. J. Murray, *The Press in the French Revolution*, Cheshire and Ginn, 1971, pp. 287–8.

## document 16
## The *armée révolutionnaire* at Pontoise

*This report by a detachment of the Parisian* armée révolutionnaire *to the general assembly of the Section of the Observatory on 16 March 1794 shows the day-to-day work of provisioning the cities, especially Paris.*

Liberty, Equality, Fraternity or Death. The Revolutionary Army at Pontoise sur l'Oise, north west of Paris. Citizens and Brothers. The citizen soldiers of the Revolutionary Army, still imbued with Revolutionary principles, are now stationed at Pontoise and assure you that they have only left Paris and their homes to thwart Intrigue and Aristocracy to the utmost. From the moment we arrived here, we have been occupied in arranging the provisioning of Paris. Several of our comrades, in the course of their duties, have found eggs and butter hidden in cupboards in farmhouses and even grain hidden in barrels.

The very mention of our name makes traitors go pale. For more than three months we have demanded the authority to exercise full surveillance. Our demands have been in vain. Our brother citizens lack everything, and if we do not have sufficient food, it is because the scarcity is only apparent. We ask that we might search households, which we have not done so far, at least only feebly. We ask that the Revolutionary Commissioners send us a true *Sans Culotte*, authorised to override the authority of the local Commune. By such means we shall foil the counter-revolutionaries who go into the countryside and buy up foodstuffs in order to sell them to the rich and selfish at inflated prices.

We ask that we be allowed to requisition food and bring it to Paris. We made such a demand to the Commission for Provisioning the Republic, but have had no reply. Now calumny directs its steps towards us; that is why we ask you to give us the chance to prove that we are still Republicans and supporters of the Mountain. We are obliged to tell you that it is the incompetence of the municipal authorities that is the sole cause of the shortage of basic necessities.

Archives Nationales, W 159.

# A justification of the Terror
**document 17**

*This speech by Saint-Just on 26 February 1794 was occasioned by demands from the Convention that reports be made on the thousands of political prisoners awaiting trial. The so-called* Indulgents *tended to believe in the innocence of many of these prisoners and Saint-Just struck back at them.*

Citizens, how could anyone delude himself that you are inhuman? Your Revolutionary Tribunal has condemned three hundred rogues to death within a year. Has not the Spanish Inquisition done worse than that, and, my God, for what a cause! Have the assizes in England slaughtered no one in that period? And what about Bender [the Prussian general], who roasts Belgian babies? What of the dungeons of Germany, where people are entombed, do you ever hear about them? What about the kings of Europe, does anyone moan to them about pity? Oh, do not allow yourselves to become soft-hearted! . . . To see the indulgence that is advocated by a few, you would think that they were the masters of our own destiny and the chief priests of freedom. Since the month of May last, our history is a lesson about the terrible extremities to which indulgence leads. In that period, Dumouriez had abandoned our conquests; patriots were being assassinated in Frankfort; Custine had abandoned Mainz, the Palatinate and the banks of the Rhine; Calvados was in revolt; the Vendée was victorious; Lyon, Bordeaux, Marseille and Toulon were in arms against the French people; Condé, Valenciennes and Le

Quesnoy had capitulated; our armies were being beaten in the Pyrenees and around Mont Blanc. You were being betrayed by everyone and it seemed as if men headed the government and the armies only to destroy them and plunder the debris. The navy was bribed, the arsenals and ships were in ashes; the currency was undermined, our banks and industries were controlled by foreigners. Yet the greatest of our misfortunes was a certain fear of the concentration of authority necessary to save the state. The conspirators of the party of the Right had blunted in advance, by an unsuspected stratagem, the weapons which you might later use to resist and punish them . . . today there are still some who would like once again to break these weapons.

C. Vellay, ed., *Oeuvres Complètes de Saint-Just*, Paris, 1908, ii, 236–7

## document 18
## The crime of indifference

*Many people tried by Revolutionary tribunals under the Terror were accused of indifference, under Article 10 of the Law of* Suspects *of 10 September 1793. Among those charged with doing nothing to advance the Revolutionary cause was Jean Sellon, a lawyer who appeared before the Marseille tribunal. Indifference was regarded as a more serious offence for a man of means and education.*

He possesses a very moderate patriotism. If he can give proof of civic responsibility, it is only by acts which are common to many people. He has never wished to take a firmly committed attitude. If he has never frequently attended the sectional assembly, it is rather out of fear of compromising himself than of wishing to serve the public good. He has allowed his knowledge and enlightenment to wallow in selfish freedom dangerous to the Republic. He cannot say that he has openly condemned the counter-revolution.

Archives départmentales, Bouches-du-Rhône, L 3118, 27 April 1794.

## document 19
## Infamous words

*Some of the charges under the Law of* Suspects *verged on the ridiculous, though taken very seriously. At Limoges, the Revolutionary tribunal called in expert opinion in the form of two writing masters to decide upon the guilt of a volunteer, Gabriel David. The experts decided that the mots* infâmes *on the leave pass were in his hand and he was found guilty and imprisoned.*

There was tried before us, in accordance with the indictment, Gabriel David, who was interrogated as follows:

Did you write 'Shit on the nation' on your leave pass?

He replied 'No'; that he did not know how the shocking words got there and did not know whose was the sacrilegious hand which had written them; that he had been taken by surprise when the commissioner for war had read them to him, that he swore once again that he was not the author and as evidence of his innocence pointed to the fact that if his leave pass had contained anything counter-revolutionary he would have consigned it to the flames rather than have shown it to the commissioner for war.

Archives départementales, Haute-Vienne, L843, 28 Messidor an II (16 July 1794).

## Apathy in lower Normandy

document 20

*This extract is from a report by Citizen Le Grand, on a mission to Normandy as an agent of the government in July 1793, especially concerned with finding supplies of food for Paris, at a time when the federalist revolt in Caen was at its zenith. He is writing to the Ministry of the Interior.*

In the area of the Auge, as in all the part of Calvados on this side of Caen, the inhabitants seem thoroughly apathetic towards the Revolution, and regard it with more curiosity than interest. One gathers from their talk that they are exhausted by the excessive increases in the price of basic necessities and, even more so, by the rarity and poor quality of bread; they have no clear opinions about anything else, they await events and pray for the restoration of order and calm. The towns of Pont L'Evêque and Honfleur, the only ones there are in these parts, share the same outlook and, up till now, have done nothing to raise levies of men . . .

Pont L'Evêque, 27 July 1793, 2nd year of the Republic. Archives Nationales, F20 170, cited by J. M. Lévy, *Annales Historiques de la Révolution Française*, vol. xxxv, 1963, p. 225.

## document 21
# The principles of Revolutionary government

*This speech, delivered by Robespierre on 25 December 1793, argued that France had not yet reached the stage where peaceful constitutional government was possible. Until France had conquered her enemies, there had to be Revolutionary government and a more severe policy of intimidation, including a speedier and more efficient Revolution tribunal.*

The theory of Revolutionary government is as new as the Revolution which has developed it . . . the function of government is to direct the moral and physical resources of the nation towards its essential aim. The aim of constitutional government is to preserve the Republic: that of Revolutionary government is to put the Republic on a secure foundation. The Revolution is the war of liberty against its enemies; the constitution is the régime of victorious and peace-loving liberty. Revolutionary government needs to be extraordinarily active, precisely because it is at war. It is subject to less uniform and rigorous rules, because the circumstances in which it finds itself are tempestuous and changing, and above all because it is obliged to employ ceaselessly new and urgent resources for new and pressing threats.

Constitutional government is primarily concerned with civil liberty: revolutionary government with public liberty. Under a constitutional régime it is more or less enough to protect individuals against abuses of government. Under a revolutionary régime the government itself is obliged to defend itself against all the factions which threaten it. Revolutionary government gives public protection to good citizens: to the enemies of the people it deals out only death . . . .

If revolutionary government has to be more active in its policies and more free in its actions than ordinary government, is it then less just and less legitimate? No: it rests on the most sacred of all laws, the safety of the people; and on the most irrefutable of all arguments: that of necessity. Revolutionary government has rules of its own, resting on the principles of justice and public order. It has no room for anarchy and disorder; its aim, on the contrary, is to repress them, in order to affirm and develop the rule of law; it has no time for the arbitrary. It is not directed by individual feelings, but by the public interest . . . It is necessary to navigate between two rocks: weakness and boldness, reaction and extremism . . .

*Archives Parlementaires*, vol. lxxxii, Paris 1913, p. 300.

# The Republic of Virtue

*Robespierre's speech of 5 February 1794 set down the moral aims of the Revolution. Revolutionary terror would lead to a new republic of virtue, where everyone would respect the nation and its laws and the sovereignty of the people.*

What is our ultimate aim? The peaceful enjoyment of liberty and equality; the reign of eternal justice, whose laws are engraved, not on marble or stone, but in the hearts of all men, even in that of the slave who forgets them and of the tyrant who rejects them. (*Applause*) We desire to see an order of things where all base and cruel feelings are suppressed, and where the law encourages beneficent and generous feelings; where ambition means the desire for glory and the service of the Republic; where social distinctions emerge from conditions of equality; where the citizen is subject to the magistrate, the magistrate to the people, and the people to the principle of justice; where the nation assures the well being of every individual and where every individual proudly enjoys the prosperity and glory of the nation; where all men's spirits are uplifted by the continual sharing of republican sentiments, and by the need to be worthy of the esteem of a great people; where the arts adorn the liberty which ennobles them; where commerce is a source of public wealth, not only of the monstrous affluence of a few families. In our country we wish to substitute morality for egoism, honesty for mere love of honour, principles for customs, duties for convention, the reign of reason for the tyranny of fashion, the fear of vice for the fear of bad luck; we want to substitute pride for insolence, magnanimity for vanity, love of glory for love of money, good men for mere good company, merit for intrigue, genius for slickness, truth for brilliance, the appeal of happiness for the boredom of sensuality, the grandeur of man for the pettiness of great men; a happy, powerful and magnanimous people for one that is amiable, frivolous and discontented. That is to say, we wish to replace the vices and follies of monarchy by the virtues and miraculous achievements of the Republic. (*Applause*) In a word, we wish to fulfil the plan of nature and promote the destiny of humanity, to fulfil the promises of enlightened philosophy, to absolve providence for a long reign of crime and tyranny. All this in order that France, formerly illustrious among enslaved countries, will eclipse the glory of all the free peoples who have ever existed and will become a model for all nations to imitate; so that France will become the scourge of oppressors, the saviour of the oppressed, the bright star of the universe; and whilst we seal our achievements with our blood, we can at least see the stars of universal happiness shining . . . that is our ambition: that is our aim.

*Archives Parlementaires*, vol. lxxxiv, Paris 1962, p. 143.

## document 23
### Revolutionary enthusiasm

*This address, sent by the* société populaire *of Bergerac, in the Dordogne, to the National Convention on 16 April 1794 after the arrest and execution of the Dantonists, provides an insight into the attitudes and activities of local militants, with their somewhat inflated sense of importance.*

Legislators – We shook with indignation when we learned that you have been surrounded by the darkest conspiracy. What! Were they trying to destroy the national government? It would have been the most pure and zealous defenders of the people who would have been the first victims! The Mountain has been polluted by conspirators! The monsters! They have suffered the fate of enemies of the nation. Your courage and determined surveillance will continue to strike such blows . . .

Destroy all factions with the same energy, annihilate all plots aiming to undermine liberty. Our Parisian brothers are there already. They will preserve the integrity of the national government. Foreigners, traitors in disguise, still circulate among them . . .

If they need assistance, we demand to be the first to be called and, as at the time of the overthrow of the monarchy, we will be the first to arrive.

Printed in H. Labroue, *La Société Populaire de Bergerac pendant la Révolution*, Paris, Librairie Rieder, 1915, p. 356.

# Glossary

*ancien régime*   Term invented in the 1790s to describe the government and way of life destroyed by the Revolution in 1789.

*armées révolutionnaires*   Citizen 'armies' of *sans culottes* raised in various regions in the autumn of 1793 whose primary tasks were to ensure the grain-supply of the cities and to enforce political orthodoxy.

*assignat*   Revolutionary paper-money, at first issued to finance the sale of church lands, but in general use after the summer of 1791.

*biens nationaux*   Confiscated property of Church, aristocracy or *suspects*, nationalised and sold by auction during the Revolution.

*bourgeois*   Carried a variety of meanings in the eighteenth century; used loosely here to mean the propertied classes below the nobility and above peasants and urban workers.

*cahiers (de doléances)*   Lists of grievances drawn up by each of the three estates or orders in towns, villages and guilds at the time of elections for the Estates-General in 1789.

*certificat de civisme*   Document attesting to the political orthodoxy of the holder; a kind of 'Revolutionary passport'.

*comités de surveillance*   'Watch' committees elected by the assemblies of the *sections*; they tended to assume powers of policing and security, as well as some local government functions. Created in April 1793. *Comités révolutionnaires* were similar.

*Commune, Paris*   Title given to the Paris local government that emerged at the City Hall (*Hôtel de Ville*) after the fall of the Bastille. The so-called 'Revolutionary Commune' aspired to function as an alternative central government in the crisis of August–September 1792. The Commune itself was abolished in August 1794.

*Cordeliers Club*   More 'plebeian' and generally more radical than the Jacobin Club (below). A product of the electoral Cordeliers district. The club functioned partly as an electoral organisation, as well as a centre for propaganda and political planning. The best known of its leaders were Marat, Danton, Hébert, Vincent and Ronsin.

*Dantonists*   Basically the friends of Danton, but, by extension, the term was also applied to the *Indulgents* or opponents of the Terror and to some businessmen and financiers, all of whom formed the Right opposition in the factional crisis of the spring of 1794.

*enragés*   A small group of extreme revolutionaries, led by Jacques Roux and Jean Varlet. Condemned by the Jacobins (below) and

Cordeliers (above), they had considerable influence over the Paris *sans culottes* in 1793.

*fédérés* Contingents of armed men sent from the provinces to Paris in 1792 to defend the capital against Austrian and Prussian attack from the north east frontier.

*Feuillants* Name given to the large group of royalist deputies and journalists who broke with the Jacobins (below) to form their own club in protest against the campaign to depose the King or suspend him from office after the Flight to Varennes in June 1791.

*Hébertists* Originally applied to the followers of Jacques-René Hébert, editor of *Le Père Duchesne* (p. 150); by extension, the term came to be applied to all groups taking part in the Left opposition to the Revolutionary government in the autumn of 1793 and the spring of 1794; among these groups were many in the Paris Commune and Ministry of War, the 'dechristianisers', the leaders of the *armées révolutionnaires* and Cordeliers Club (above).

*intendants* Provincial agents of the royal administration before 1789.

*Jacobins, Jacobin Club* Name assumed by the former members of the Breton Club when they established themselves in the former Jacobin Convent in Paris in October 1789. The Club went through a series of transformations through the secession of the Feuillants (above) (June 1791) and successive purges of Girondins, Dantonists (above) and Hébertists (above) and ended up in the summer of 1794 as the group devoted to Robespierre. Dissolved in November 1794.

*journées* The great 'Revolutionary Days', such as 14 July 1789 or 10 August 1792, involving popular insurrection.

*livre* (later *franc*) In 1789 equivalent to 1s.8d. sterling. There were 20 *sous* (or *sols*) to a *livre*.

*Maximum* There were two laws of the *Maximum*: that of May 1793, imposing a limit on the price of grain and flour only; and that of September 1793, extending price control to basic necessities and freezing wage levels.

*menu peuple* ('little people') The common people.

*National Guard (milice bourgeoise)* Citizens' army, or militia, originally raised by the Paris districts in July 1789.

*parlements* Thirteen law courts composed of noble magistrates which exercised judicial powers and the right to register royal decrees before 1789; they saw themselves as a (non-elected) brake on 'absolutism'. The *parlement* of Paris had jurisdiction over nearly two-thirds of France. Not 'parliaments' in the English sense.

*pauvre bougre* 'Poor decent fellow' (*not* the English 'bugger').

*'Père Duchesne'* Hébert's scurrilous, vitriolic and obscene newspaper; the favourite reading of the *sans culottes*; applied also as Hébert's nickname, for the paper was ostensibly written by an irascible *sans culotte*, often identified with Hébert himself.

*représentants en mission* Members of the Convention sent to the provinces and the armies in 1793 with full administrative powers to boost conscription, the war effort and revolutionary fervour.

*sections* The forty-eight units into which Paris was divided for electoral and general political purposes by a municipal law of May–June 1790. Dominated by the *sans culottes*, they had various names, such as *Droit-des-Hommes*, *Arsenal*, *Bonnet-Rouge* and *l'Homme-Armé*.

*seigneurs* Landlords with feudal rights over their tenants (vassals).

*suspects* Term in use from August 1792 for persons suspected of harbouring treasonable designs against the Revolution. In September 1793 a Law of *Suspects* was introduced, enabling such persons to be arrested and brought before the Revolutionary Tribunal. This marked the official opening of the 'Great Terror'.

*taxation populaire* Price control by crowd action, usually involving the seizure and sale of goods at a 'fair' or 'just' price.

*terroriste* (terrorist) A supporter of the Terror of 1793–94. Though some of them committed bloody deeds, they are not to be confused with 'terrorists' in the modern sense.

*Thermidor* The month in the Revolutionary calendar running from 19 July–7 August. Applied here to the two days in Thermidor (9th and 10th) of the Year II which saw the overthrow of Robespierre and his associates. Hence the use of the term *Thermidorians* to describe Robespierre's immediate successors.

*vertu* (virtue) Used here, as by Robespierre, in the sense of civic virtue (that is, love of France and the Revolution, or loyalty to the Jacobin cause) rather than in the sense of private morality or virtuous conduct in personal relations.

*Year II* (*an II*) The second year of the French Republic (22 September 1793 to 21 September 1794). Most often applied to the period of office of the great Committee of Public Safety (July 1793–July 1794). Also the year of the Great Terror.

# Chronological Summary

| 1786 | Aug | Calonne's land tax proposals |
|------|-----|------------------------------|
| 1787 | Feb | Assembly of the Notables |
| | May | Brienne succeeded Calonne; dismissal of the Notables |
| 1788 | May–July | Suspension of the *Parlements*; 'revolt of the nobility' |
| | Aug–Sept | Brienne succeeded by Necker; *Parlements* recalled |
| 1789 | April | Riots in Paris and the provinces |
| | May | States-General met |
| | June | Tennis Court Oath: Royal Session |
| | July | Dismissal of Necker; fall of the Bastille; the 'Great Fear' |
| | Aug | Abolition of feudal rights; Declaration of Rights |
| | Sept | Defeat of the *monarchiens* |
| | Oct | March to Versailles |
| | Nov | Decrees on the Church, local government and *assignats* |
| 1790 | Feb–Mar | Religious conflict in Nîmes |
| | June | Abolition of the nobility |
| | July | Civil Constitution of the Clergy |
| | Nov | Enforcement of the clerical oath |
| 1791 | June | Flight to Varennes |
| | July | Massacre on the Champ de Mars |
| | Aug | Declaration of Pillnitz |
| | Sept | King accepted the Constitution and the Constituent Assembly dissolved |
| | Oct | Meeting of the Legislative Assembly |
| 1792 | April | Declaration of war with Austria |
| | June | First invasion of the Tuileries |
| | July | Brunswick Manifesto and agitation in the Paris *sections* |
| | Aug | Revolution of 10 August and suspension of the King; Beginning of the 'First Terror' |
| | Sept | Fall of Verdun; September Massacres; Battle of Valmy; meeting of the Convention; abolition of |

|      |       | the monarchy and beginning of the Year I of the Republic |
|------|-------|----------------------------------------------------------|
|      | Nov   | Battle of Jemappes; French armies into Belgium |
|      | Dec   | Trial of the King |
| 1793 | Jan   | Execution of Louis XVI |
|      | Feb   | War with England; food riots in Paris; the *enragés* |
|      | March | War with Spain; outbreak of revolt in La Vendée |
|      | April | Establishment of the Committee of Public Safety; first *maximum* (grain) |
|      | May   | Federalist revolts at Lyon, Marseille, Caen and Bordeaux |
|      | June  | Fall of the Girondins; Jacobin Constitution of 1793 |
|      | July  | Robespierre entered the Committee of Public Safety |
|      | Aug   | *Levée en masse;* surrender of Toulon to the English |
|      | Sept  | Beginning of Year II of the Republic; Terror 'the order of the day'; law of *suspects*; general *maximum*; creation of the Parisian *armée révolutionnaire* |
|      | Oct   | Government declared 'Revolutionary until the peace'; recapture of Lyon by Republican forces; trial and execution of the Girondins |
|      | Nov   | Festival of Reason |
|      | Dec   | Reorganisation of Revolutionary Government by the law of 14 Frimaire; defeat of the Vendée rebels; English evacuated Toulon |
| 1794 | Feb   | Laws of Ventôse |
|      | March | Arrest of the Hébertists and Dantonists |
|      | May   | Attempts to assassinate Robespierre |
|      | June  | Festival of the Supreme Being |
|      | July  | Maximum wage legislation; arrest and execution of Robespierre and his followers |
|      | Nov   | Jacobin Club closed |
|      | Dec   | Abolition of the *maximum* |
| 1795 | April | Rising of Germinal |
|      | May   | Rising of Prairial |
|      | August| Constitution of the Year III |
|      | Oct   | Rising of Vendémiaire; dissolution of the Convention and the beginning of the Directory |

# Bibliography

*The literature on the French Revolution is immense and what follows is necessarily a personal and therefore partial selection, with some bias towards works in English. The place of publication is London unless otherwise indicated.*

DOCUMENTS
*While there are massive French collections of documentary material, relatively few of them are available to English readers outside major academic libraries. The following may be consulted (texts are in French unless otherwise stated).*

1   Thompson, J. M. *French Revolution Documents 1789–94*, Oxford: Blackwell, 1933.

2   Roberts J. M. *French Revolution Documents*, i, 1966; vol. ii, ed. Hardman, J., 1974; Oxford: Blackwell.

3   Hardman, J. *The French Revolution 1785–1795*, Edward Arnold, 1981. A selection of documents in English, with linking commentary. Mainly political and constitutional.

4   Stewart, J. H. *A Documentary Survey of the French Revolution*, New York: Macmillan, 1951.

5   Gershoy, L. *The Era of the French Revolution 1789–99*, Anvil Books, 1958.

6   Markov, W. and Soboul, A. *Die Sansculotten von Paris*, East Berlin: Akademie-Verlag, 1957, prints documents in French and German parallel texts.

7   Gilchrest, J. and Murray, W. T. *The Press in the French Revolution*, Ginn, 1971, translates extracts from the Paris press between 1789 and 1794.

BOOKS AND ARTICLES
*The French Revolution is placed in its European context by:*

8   Lefebvre, G. 'La Révolution francaise dans l'histoire du monde', *Annales*, 1948.

9   Hufton, O. *Europe: Privilege and Protest 1730–1789*, Fontana, 1980.

10  Rudé, G. *Revolutionary Europe 1783–1815*, Fontana, 1964.

11  Rudé, G. *Europe in the Eighteenth Century*, Weidenfeld & Nicolson, 1972.

12  Ford, F. L. *Europe 1780–1830*, Longman, 1970.

13  Hobsbawm, E. J. *The Age of Revolution 1789–1848*, Weidenfeld & Nicolson, 1962.

**14** Goodwin, A., ed. *The American and French Revolutions 1763–93* vol. viii of *The New Cambridge Modern History*, Cambridge: Cambridge U.P., 1965, introduction.

*Two books which argue the thesis of the 'Atlantic Revolution' are:*
**15** Palmer, R. R. *The Age of the Democratic Revolution*, 2 vols, Princeton, N.J.: Princeton U.P., 1959, 1964 (paperback 1969).
**16** Godechot, J. *Les Révolutions 1770–1799*, 'Nouvelle Clio' 36, P.U.F.: Paris, 1963. The narrative sections have been translated as *France and the Atlantic Revolution of the Eighteenth Century*, New York: Collier-Macmillan, 1971.

*See also:*
**17** Cobban, A. 'The Age of the Democratic Revolution', *History*, clv, 1960.

*For good introductory surveys of the French Revolution see:*
**18** Goodwin, A. *The French Revolution*, Hutchinson, 1953.
**19** Hampson, N. *A Social History of the French Revolution*, RKP, 1963.
**20** Hampson, N. *The French Revolution: A Concise History*, Thames & Hudson, 1975.
**21** Sydenham, M. J. *The French Revolution*, Batsford, 1965.

*Among larger studies of the Revolution are:*
**22** Lefebvre, G. *La Révolution française*, Paris: P.U.F., 6th ed. 1968. Translated in two volumes: *The French Revolution from its Origins to 1793*; *The French Revolution from 1793–1799*, RKP, 1962, 1964.
**23** Furet, F. and Richet, D. *The French Revolution* [1965], translation Weidenfeld & Nicolson, 1970.
**24** Sutherland, D. M. G. *France 1789–1815: Revolution and Counter-Revolution*, Fontana/Collins, 1985.
**25** Hampson, N. *Prelude to Terror: The Constituent Assembly and the failure of consensus 1789–91*, Oxford: Blackwell, 1988.
**26** Hampson, N. *The First European Revolution 1776–1815*, Thames & Hudson, 1969.

*For the historiography of the Revolution see* **16**, *part ii, the introductions of* **45**, **62**, *below and:*
**27** Geyl, P. *Encounters in History*, Fontana, 1967, part ii, ch. 2.
**28** Cobban, A. *Historians and the Causes of the French Revolution*, Historical Association pamphlet G2, 1958.

**29** Cobban, A. *Aspects of the French Revolution*, Jonathan Cape, 1968. Reprints **28**.

**30** Rudé, G. *Interpretations of the French Revolution*, Historical Association pamphlet G47, 1961.

**31** McManners, J. 'The historiography of the French Revolution', ch. xxii in **14**.

**32** Goodwin, A. 'The recent historiography of the French Revolution', in Moody, T. W., ed., *Historical Studies VI*, RKP, 1968.

**33** Cobb, R. C. *Modern French History in Britain*, British Academy/Oxford U.P., 1974.

**34** Furet, F. *La gauche et la Révolution française au milieu du xix^e siècle*, Paris: Hachette, 1986.

*For criticisms of the French Jacobin-Marxist school, which views the Revolution as a class struggle and the victory of the bourgeoisie over 'feudalism' see* **23**, **24** *above and:*

**35** Cobban, A. *The Social Interpretation of the French Revolution*, Cambridge: Cambridge U.P., 1964.

**36** Behrens, B. 'Professor Cobban and his critic', *Historical Journal*, ix, 1966.

**37** Behrens, B. ' "Straight" history and "History in depth" ', *ibid.* vii, 1965.

**38** Taylor, G. V. 'Types of capitalism in eighteenth-century France', *English Historical Review*, lxxix, 1964.

**39** Taylor, G. V. 'Noncapitalist wealth and the origins of the French Revolution', *American Historical Review*, lxxii, 1967.

**40** Kaplow, J., Shapiro, G. and Eisenstein, E. L. 'Class in the French Revolution', *American Historical Review*, lxxii, 1967.

**41** Palmer, R. R. 'Sur le rôle de la bourgeoisie dans la Révolution française', *Annales Historiques de la Révolution française* [hereafter *AHRF*], 1967.

**42** Kaplow, J. ed., *New Perspectives on the French Revolution*, New York: Wiley, 1965.

**43** Furet, F. *Penser la Révolution française*, Paris: Gallimard, 1978; translation: *Interpreting the French Revolution*, Cambridge: Cambridge U.P. 1981.

**44** Ellis, G. 'The "Marxist Interpretation" of the French Revolution', *English Historical* Review, xciii, 1978.

**45** Blanning, T. C. W. *The French Revolution: Aristocrats versus Bourgeois?* Macmillan, 1987.

**46** Lewis, G. *Life in Revolutionary France*, Batsford, 1972.

Bibliography

On the ancien régime, *see* **9**, **11**, **14** *above and:*
47  Doyle, W. *The Ancien Regime*, Macmillan, 1986.
48  Shennan, J. H. *France before the Revolution*, Methuen, 1983.
49  Behrens, C. B. A. *The Ancien Regime*, Thames & Hudson, 1967.
50  Sagnac, P. *La formation de la société française moderne*, vol. ii, Paris: P.U.F., 1947.
51  Sagnac, P. 'La crise de l'économie française à la fin de l'ancien régime et au début de la Révolution', *Revue d'Histoire Economique et Sociale*, iii, 1950.
52  McManners, J. 'France' in Goodwin, A. ed., *The European Nobility in the Eighteenth Century*, Black, 1953.
53  Dakin, D. 'The Breakdown of the old regime in France', ch. xxi in **14** above.

*Among a vast number of local studies are:*
54  Lefebvre, G. 'Urban society in the Orléanais in the eighteenth century,' *Past and Present*, 19, 1961.
55  Forster, R. *The Nobility of Toulouse in the Eighteenth Century*, Oxford U.P., 1960.
56  Godechot, J. and Moncassin, S. 'Les structures sociales de Toulouse en 1749 et en 1785', *AHRF*, 1965.
57  Kaplow, J. *Elbeuf during the Revolutionary Period*, Baltimore, Md: Johns Hopkins U.P., 1964.
58  Hufton, O. H. *Bayeux in the late Eighteenth Century*, Oxford: Oxford U.P., 1967.
59  Le Goff, T. J. A. *Vannes and its Region*, Oxford: Oxford U.P., 1981.
60  McManners, J. *French Ecclesiastical Society under the Ancien Regime: a study of Angers*, Manchester: Manchester U.P., 1960.

*For the 'Pre-Revolution' of 1787–89 see* **25** *above and:*
61  Lefebvre, G. *The Coming of the French Revolution*, Princeton, N. J.: Princeton U.P., 1947; translation of *Quatre-Vingt-Neuf*, Paris, 1939.
62  Doyle, W. *Origins of the French Revolution*, Oxford: Oxford U.P., 1980.
63  Egret, J. *The French Revolution 1787–88* [1962], translation Chicago: Chicago U.P., 1977.
64  Egret, J. 'Les origines de la Revolution en Bretagne 1788–89', *Revue Historique*, ccxiii, 1955.
65  Egret, J. 'La pré-révolution en Provence 1787–1789', *AHRF*, 1954.

**66** Lemoigne, Y. 'Population and Provisions in Strasbourg in the eighteenth century'; and

**67** Trenard, L. 'The Social Crisis in Lyons on the eve of the French Revolution' are translated in **42** above, as are **64** and **65.**

**68** Goodwin, A. 'Calonne, the Assembly of the French Notables of 1787 and the origins of the '*Révolte Nobiliaire*', *English Historical Review*, lxi, 1946.

**69** Rudé, G. 'The outbreak of the French Revolution', *Past and Present*, 8, 1955.

**70** Gruder, V. 'Paths to political consciousness: the Assembly of the Notables of 1787 and the "Pre-Revolution" in France', *French Historical Studies*, xiii, 1984.

**71** Hunt, L. A. *Revolution and Urban Politics in Provincial France: Troyes and Rheims 1786–90*, Stanford U.P., 1978.

**72** Greenlaw, R. W. 'Pamphlet literature in France during the period of the aristocratic revolt', *Journal of Modern History*, xxi, 1957.

**73** Doyle, W. 'The Parlements of France and the breakdown of the old regime', *French Historical Studies*, vi, 1970.

**74** Doyle, W. *The Parlement of Bordeaux 1771–90*, Benn, 1974.

**75** Stone, B. *The Parlement of Paris 1774–89*, Raleigh: University of North Carolina Press, 1981.

**76** Chaussinand-Nogaret, G. *The French Nobility in the Eighteenth Century* [1976], translated Cambridge: Cambridge U.P., 1985.

**77** Chaussinand-Nogaret, G. *Une histoire des élites 1780–1848*, Paris: Mouton, 1975.

**78** Behrens, B. 'Nobles, privileges and taxes in France at the end of the *ancien régime*', *Economic History Review*, xv, 1962–3.

**79** Harris, R. D. 'French finances and the American War 1777–83', *Journal of Modern History*, xlviii, 1976.

**80** Lucas, C. 'Nobles, bourgeois and the origins of the French Revolution', *Past and Present*, 60, 1973.


*On the economy in the 1780s see* **45, 47, 51** *above and:*

**81** Labrousse, E. *Crise de l'économie française à la fin de l'ancien régime et au début de la Révolution*, Paris: P.U.F., 1944.

**82** Reddy, W. M. *The Rise of Market Culture: the textile trade and French society 1750–1900*, Cambridge: Cambridge U.P., 1984.

**83** Gullickson, G. L. *Spinners and Weavers of Auffay*, Cambridge: Cambridge U.P., 1987.

**84** Greenlaw, R. W. ed., *Economic Origins of the French Revolution: poverty or prosperity?* Heath/Harrap, 1958.

*There is a substantial literature on the French Enlightenment and its impact. See* **25**, **26**, *and* **62** *(ch. 4) above and:*
**85** Hampson, N. *The Enlightenment,* Penguin, 1968.
**86** Hampson, N. *Will and Circumstance: Montesquieu, Rousseau and the French Revolution,* Duckworth, 1983.
**87** Cobban, A. 'The Enlightenment and the French Revolution' in **29** above.
**88** Richet, D. 'Autours des origines idéologiques lointaines de la Révolution française', *Annales,* 1969.
**89** Darnton, R. 'The high Enlightenment and the low life of literature in pre-revolutionary France', *Past and Present,* 51, 1971.
**90** Darnton, R. *The Business of Enlightenment: a publishing history of the* Encyclopédie *1775–1800,* Cambridge, Mass.: Harvard U.P., 1979.
**91** Darnton, R. *The Literary Underground of the Old Regime,* Cambridge, Mass.: Harvard U.P., 1982.
**92** Darnton, R. *The Great Cat Massacre,* Allen Lane, 1984.
**93** Furet, F. and Sachs, W. 'La croissance de l'alphabétisation en France, xviiie–xixe siècles', *Annales,* 1974.
**94** Hampson, N. *The French Revolution and Democracy,* Reading: Reading U.P., 1983.

*For popular movements from 1775 and the importance of bread prices, see* **63** *above and:*
**95** Doyle, W. 'Was there an aristocratic reaction in pre-revolutionary France?', *Past and Present,* 57, 1972.
**96** Rudé, G. *The Crowd in the French Revolution,* Oxford: Oxford U.P., 1979.
**97** Rudé, G. *Paris and London in the Eighteenth Century,* Fontana, 1970.
**98** Lefebvre, G. 'Le mouvement des prix et les origines de la Révolution française', *AHRF,* 1937.
**99** Rose, R. B. 'Tax revolt and popular organization in Brittany', *Past and Present,* 43, 1969.

*For the events of 1789 prior to 14 July see* **25**, **61**, **62**, **69** *above and:*
**100** Godechot, J. *The Taking of the Bastille* [1965], translation Faber, 1970.

**101** Lefebvre, G. 'Foules révolutionnaires', *AHRF*, 1934, translation in **40** above.

**102** Egret, J. *La Révolution des Notables: Mounier et les Monarchiens*, Paris; Armand Colin, 1950.

**103** Hutt, M. G. 'The role of the curés in the Estates-General of 1789', *Journal of Ecclesiastical History*, vi, 1955.

**104** Necheles, R. F. 'The curés in the Estates-General of 1789', *Journal of Modern History*, xlvi, 1974.

**105** Forsyth, M. *Reason and Revolution: the political thought of the Abbé Sieyès*, Leicester: Leicester U.P., 1987.

**106** Rudé, G. 'The Fall of the Bastille', *History Today*, iv, 1954, reprinted in **97**.

**107** Lefebvre, G. 'La Révolution française et les paysans', *AHRF*, 1933.

**108** Rudé, G. 'La composition sociale des insurrections parisiennes de 1789 à 1791', *AHRF*, 1952, translated in **97** above.

**109** Scott, S. A. *The Response of the Royal Army to the French Revolution*, Oxford: Oxford U.P., 1978.

**110** Murphy, T. and Higgonet, P. 'Les députés de la noblesse aux États-Généraux de 1789', *Revue d'Histoire Moderne et Contemporaine*, xx, 1973.

**111** Wick, D. 'The court nobility and the French Revolution: the example of the Committee of Thirty', *Eighteenth Century Studies*, 13, 1980.

**112** Caron, P. 'La tentative de contre-révolution de juin-juillet 1789'. *Revue d'histoire moderne*, viii, 1906–7.

*On the peasant insurrection, the 'Great Fear' and the municipal revolution see* **61** *(ch. 10) and:*

**113** Lefebvre, G. *The Great Fear of 1789* [1932], translation New Left Books, 1973.

**114** Davies, A. 'The origins of the French peasant revolution of 1789', *History*, xlix, 1964.

**115** Ligou, D. 'A propos de la Révolution municipale', *Revue d'Histoire Économique et Sociale*, xxxviii, 1960.

**116** Hunt, L. A. 'Committees and Communes: local politics and national revolution in 1789', *Comparative Studies in History and Society*, xviii, 1976.

*For the political conflicts of August and September 1789 and the October Days, see* **24** *(ch. 2),* **25**, **101**, **102** *above and:*

**117** Mathiez, A. 'Étude critique sur les journées de 5 et 6 Octobre 1789', *Revue Historique*, lxviii-lxix, 1898–1900.

Bibliography

**118** Bradby, E. D. *Barnave*, Oxford: Oxford U.P., 1915.
**119** Roberts, J. M. *The French Revolution*, Oxford: Oxford U.P., 1978, ch. 2.
**120** Freddi, F. 'La presse parisienne et la nuit du 4 août', *AHRF*, 259, 1985.

*On the Church see:*
**121** McManners, J. *The French Revolution and the Church*, SPCK, 1969.
**122** Tackett, T. *Priest and Parish in Eighteenth Century France: a social and political study of the curés in a diocese* [Gap] *of Dauphiné*, Princeton, N. J.: Princeton U.P., 1977.
**123** Vovelle, M. *Piété baroque et déchristianisation en Provence au XVIIIe siècle*, Aix-en-Provence, 1973.
**124** Hufton, O. 'The reconstruction of a church 1796–1801' in Lewis, G. and Lucas, C. eds., *Beyond the Terror*, Cambridge: Cambridge U.P., 1983.

*For the work of the Constituent Assembly and rivalries in the Legislative Assemblies see:*
**125** Le May, E. 'La composition de l'Assemblée nationale constituente', *Revue d'Histoire Moderne et Contemporaine*, xxiv, 1977.
**126** Harris, S. E. *The Assignats*, Cambridge, Mass: Harvard U.P., 1930.
**127** Godechot, J. *Les Institutions de la France sous la Révolution et L'Empire*, Paris: P.U.F., 1968.
**128** Thompson, E. *Popular Sovereignty and the French Constituent Assembly*, Manchester: Manchester U.P., 1952.
**129** Michon, G. *Essai sur l'histoire du parti Feuillant: Adrien Duport*, Paris: Puyot, 1924.
**130** Brinton, C. C. *The Jacobins* [1930], New York: Russell, 1961.
**131** Kennedy, M. *The Jacobin Clubs in the French Revolution*, Princeton, N. J.: Princeton U.P., 1981.
**132** Scott, S. F. 'Problems of law and order during 1790, the 'peaceful' year of the French Revolution', *American Historical Review*, lxxx, 1975.
**133** Mitchell, C. J. 'Political divisions within the Legislative Assembly of 1791', *French Historical Studies*, xiii, 1984.
**134** Censer, J. R. *Prelude to Power: the Parisian Radical Press 1789–91*, Baltimore, Md.: Johns Hopkins U.P., 1976.

*For the origins of the war and counter-revolution, see:*

**135** Blanning, T. C. W. *The Origins of the French Revolutionary Wars*, Longman, 1986.

**136** Blanning, T. C. W. *The French Revolution in Germany*, Oxford: Oxford U.P., 1983.

**137** Biro, S. G. *The German Policy of Revolutionary France*, Cambridge, Mass.: Harvard U.P., 1957.

**138** Godechot, J. *The Counter-Revolution 1789–1804*, RKP, 1972.

**139** Tilly, C. *The Vendée*, Cambridge, Mass.: Harvard U.P./ Arnold, 1964.

**140** Bois, P. *Les Paysans de l'Ouest*, Le Mans: Vilaire, 1960.

**141** Sutherland, D. M. G. *The Chouans: the social origins of popular counter-revolution in Upper Brittany*, Oxford: Oxford U.P., 1982.

**142** Lewis, G. *The Second Vendée; the continuity of counter-revolution in the department of the Gard 1789–1815*, Oxford: Oxford U.P., 1978.

**143** Hutt, M. *Chouannerie and Counter-Revolution*, 2 vols, Cambridge: Cambridge U.P., 1984.

**144** Johnson, H. C. *The Midi in Revolution 1789–93*, Princeton, N.J.: Princeton U.P., 1986.

**145** Hood, J. N. 'Protestant and Catholic relations and the roots of the first popular counter-revolutionary movement in France', *Journal of Modern History*, xlii, 1971.

**146** Hood, J. N. 'Revival and mutation of old rivalries in Revolutionary France', *Past and Present*, 82, 1970.

**147** Lucas, C. 'The problem of the Midi in the French Revolution', *Transactions of the Royal Historical Society*, 5th series, xxviii, 1978.

**148** Mitchell, H. 'The Vendée and Counter-Revolution', *French Historical Studies*, v, 1968.

**149** Le Goff, T. J. A. and Sutherland, D. M. G. 'The social origins of Counter-Revolution in Western France', *Past and Present*, 99, 1983.

**150** Chaumié, J. *Le Réseau d'Antraigues et la Contre-Révolution 1791– 93*, Paris: Gallimard, 1965.

**151** Balzac, Honoré de, *The Chouans*, translation Penguin Books, 1972.

*For the flight to Varennes, the Champ de Mars and the fall of the monarchy, see **96** (chs 6, 7); **24** (ch. 4) and:*

**152** Reinhard, M. *La Chute de la Royauté: 10 Août 1792*, Paris: Gallimard, 1969.

# Bibliography

**153** Vovelle, M. *The Fall of the Monarchy 1787–92* [1972] translation Cambridge: Cambridge U.P., 1981.

**154** Sydenham, M. *The Girondins*, Athlone Press, 1961.

**155** Patrick, A. 'Political divisions in the French National Convention 1792–93', *Journal of Modern History*, xli, 1969.

**156** Patrick, A. *The Men of the First French Republic: Political Alignments in the National Convention of 1792*, Baltimore, Md.: Johns Hopkins U.P., 1972.

**157** Sydenham, M. J. 'The Montagnards and their opponents', *Journal of Modern History*, xliii, 1971.

*On the* sans culottes *see* **6** *(documents),* **46** *(ch. 5) and:*

**158** Rose, R. B. *The Making of the Sans Culottes: Democratic Ideas and Institutions in Paris 1789–92*, Manchester: Manchester U.P., 1982.

**159** Soboul, A. *The Parisian Sans Culottes and the French Revolution*, Oxford: U.P., 1964.

**160** Soboul, A. *Paysans, Sans-culottes et Jacobins*, Paris: Clavreuil, 1965.

**161** Cobb, R. C. *Les armées révolutionnaires: instrument de la Terreur dans les départements*, 2 vols, Paris: Mouton, 1961–63. Translated as *The People's Armies*. New Haven, Conn.: Yale U.P, 1987.

**162** Cobb, R. C. *Terreur et Subsistances*, Paris: Clavreuil, 1965.

**163** Cobb, R. C. *The Police and the People: French Popular Protest 1789–1820*, Oxford: Oxford U.P., 1970.

**164** Cobb, R. C. *Reactions to the French Revolution*, Oxford: Oxford U.P., 1972.

**165** Williams, G. A. *Artisans and Sans-Culottes*, Edward Arnold, 1968.

**166** Rose, R. B. 'Nursery of sans-culottes: the Société Patriotique of the Luxembourg Section 1792–95', *Bulletin of the John Rylands Library*, lxiv, 1981.

**167** Cobb, R. C. 'The Revolutionary mentality in France 1793–94', *History*, xlii, 1957.

**168** Slavin, M. L. *The French Revolution in Miniature: Section Droits-des-Hommes 1789–95*, Princeton, N.J.: Princeton U.P., 1974.

*For the 'First Terror' and the September Massacres see:*

**169** Caron, P. *La Première Terreur*, Paris: P.U.F., 1950.

**170** Caron, P. *Les massacres de Septembre*, Paris: Maison du Livre Francais, 1935.

*On the crisis of February–June 1793, see above* **96**, **154** *and:*

**171** Mathiez, A. *La vie chère et le Mouvement social sous la Terreur*, Paris: Armand Colin, 1927.

**172** Rude, G. 'Les émeutes des 25, 26 février 1793', *AHRF*, 1960.

**173** Markov, W. 'Les Jacquesroutins', *AHRF, 1960.*

**174** Rose, R. B. *The Enragés: Socialists of the French Revolution?*, Melbourne: Melbourne U.P., 1965.

**175** Cobb, R. C. *A Second Identity*, Oxford: Oxford U.P. 1969.

**176** Hufton, O. 'Women in Revolution 1780–96', *Past and Present*, 53, 1971.

**177** Phillips, R. *Family Breakdown in late eighteenth-century France: Divorce in Rouen 1792–1803*, Oxford: Oxford U.P., 1981.

**178** Jordan, D. P. *The King's Trial; the French Revolution versus Louis XVI*, Berkeley: California U.P., 1979.

*For the counter-revolutionary Federalist revolt see:*

**179** Forrest, A. *Society and Politics in Revolutionary Bordeaux*, Oxford: Oxford U.P., 1975.

**180** Edmonds, B. 'Federalism and the Urban Revolution in France in 1793', *Journal of Modern History*, lv, 1983.

**181** Lyons, M. 'The Jacobin elite of Toulouse', *European Studies Review*, vii, 1977.

**182** Crook, M. N. 'Federalism and the French Revolution: the Revolt of Toulon in 1793', *History*, lxv, 1980.

**183** Tilly, C. 'Local conflicts in the Vendée before the rebellion of 1793', *French Historical Studies*, ii, 1961.

**184** Goodwin, A. 'Counter-Revolution in Brittany', *Bulletin of the John Rylands Library*, xxxix, 1957.

**185** Goodwin, A. 'The Federalist Movement in Caen during the French Revolution', *Ibid.* xlii, 1960.

**186** Slavin, M. L. *The Making of an Insurrection*, Cambridge, Mass.: Harvard U.P., 1987.

*The literature on the Terror is massive, but see* **159–162** *above and:*

**187** Hampson, N. *The Terror in the French Revolution*, Historical Association pamphlet GS 103, 1981.

**188** Bouloiseau, M. *The Jacobin Republic* 1792–94 [1972], translation Cambridge: Cambridge U.P., 1984.

**189** Palmer, R. R. *Twelve Who Ruled*, Princeton, N. J.: Princeton U.P., 1941.

**190** Bouloiseau, M. *Le comité de salut public*, new ed., 'Que sais-je?' Paris; P.U.F., 1968.

*Bibliography*

**191** Lucas, C. *The Structure of the Terror*, Oxford: Oxford U.P., 1973.

**192** Scott, W. *Terror and Repression in Revolutionary Marseilles*, Macmillan, 1973.

**193** Gough, H. 'Politics and power: the triumph of Jacobinism at Strasbourg 1791–93', *Historical Journal*, 23, 1980.

**194** Greer, D. *The Incidence of the Terror in the French Revolution*, Cambridge, Mass.: Harvard U.P., 1935.

**195** Soboul, A. 'Une commune rurale pendant la Révolution' [Authieux], reprinted in **160**.

**196** Aubert, G. 'La Révolution à Douai', *AHRF*, 1936.

**197** Lucas, C. 'La brève carrière du terroriste Jean-Marie Lapalus', *AHRF*, 1968.

**198** Hohl, C. *Un Agent du Comité de Sûreté Générale: Nicolas Guénot*, Paris; Bibliothéque Nationale, 1968.

**199** Boucher, P. *Charles Cochon de Lapparent*, Paris: Picard, 1969.

**200** Harris, J. 'The Red Cap of Liberty: a study of dress worn by French Revolutionary partisans 1789–94', *Eighteenth Century Studies*, 14, 1981.

**201** Hunt, L. *Politics, Culture and Class in the French Revolution*, Berkeley: California U.P., 1984; Methuen, 1986.

**202** Ozouf, M. *Festivals and Revolution 1789–99* [1976], translation Cambridge, Mass.: Harvard U.P., 1988.

**203** Jones, P. M. *Politics and Rural Society: the Southern Massif Central 1750–1880*, Cambridge: Cambridge U.P., 1986.

**204** Plongeron, B. *Conscience réligieuse en la Révolution*, Paris; Picard, 1969.

**205** Mathiez, A. 'L'argenterie des églises en l'an II', *AHRF*, 1925.

**206** Soboul, A. 'Sentiment religieux et cultes populaires: sociétiés patriotiques et martyrs de la liberté', *AHRF*, 1957.

**207** Cobb, R. C. 'Les débuts de la déchristianisation à Dieppe', *AHRF*, 1970.

**208** Paillard, Y. G. 'Fanatiques et patriots dans le Puy-de-Dôme', *AHRF*, 1970.

**209** Special number of *AHRF*, 1978, for articles on dechristianisation.

**210** Vovelle, M. *Religion et Révolution. La déchristianisation de l'an II*, Paris, P.U.F.

*For the 'Reign of Virtue' see:*

**211** Mathiez, A. 'La Terreur: instrument de politique sociale des Robespierristes', *AHRF*, 1928.

212  Mathiez, A. *Études sur Robespierre*, Paris: Editions Sociales, 1958.

213  Cobban, A. 'The Fundamental Ideas of Robespierre, *English Historical Review*, 1948, reprinted in **29** above.

214  Soboul, A. 'Robespierre et les sociétés populaires', *AHRF*, 1958.

215  Soboul, A. 'Robespierre et la formation du gouvernement révolutionnaire', *Revue d'Histoire Moderne et Contemporaine*, 1958.

216  Theuriot, F. 'La conception robespierriste du bonheur', *AHRF*, 1968.

217  Hampson, N. Essays on Robespierre and Saint-Just in **86**.

*On the final phase of the Jacobin dictatorship, see:*

218  Lyons, M. 'The 9 Thermidor, Motives and Effects', *European Studies Review*, v, 1975.

219  Bienvenu, R. *The Fall of Robespierre: the Ninth of Thermidor*, Oxford: Oxford U.P., 1968.

220  Mathiez, A. 'La division des comités gouvernementaires à la veille du 9 thermidor', *Revue Historique*, 1915.

221  Mathiez, A. 'La réorganisation du gouvernement révolutionnaire, germinal-floréal an II', *AHRF*, 1927.

222  Lefebvre, G. 'Sur la loi du 22 prairial', *AHRF*, 1951, reprinted in **8** above.

223  Rudé, G. and Soboul, A. 'Le maximum des salaires Parisiens et le 9 thermidor', *AHRF*, 1954. Reprinted in **160**.

224  Eudes, M. 'La loi du prairial', *AHRF*, 1983.

225  Walter, G. *La conjuration du neuf thermidor, 24 juillet 1794*, Paris: Gallimard, 1974.

226  Rose, R. B. 'The "Red Scare" of the 1790s: the French Revolution and the "Agrarian Law"', *Past and Present*, 103, 1984.

*On the Thermidorian reaction and the White Terror, see* **23** *book ii;* **163** *section ii, part ii, and:*

227  Woronoff, D. *The Thermidorian Regime and the Directory 1794–99* [1972], translation Cambridge: Cambridge U.P., 1984.

228  Lyons, M. *France Under the Directory*, Cambridge: Cambridge U.P., 1975.

229  Tonnesson, C. *La Défaite des Sans-Culottes*, Oslo and Paris; Clavreuil, 1959.

230  Schlumberger, M. 'La reaction thermidorienne à Toulouse', *AHRF*, 1971.

**231** Woloch, I. *Jacobin Legacy: The Democratic Movement under the Directory*, Princeton, N. J.: Princeton U.P., 1971.

**232** Cobb, R. C. *Death in Paris 1795–1801*, Oxford: Oxford U.P., 1978.

*Among the countless biographies of Revolutionary leaders are:*

**233** Chaussinand-Nogaret, G. *Mirabeau*, Paris: Seuil, 1982.

**234** Hampson, N. *Danton*, Duckworth, 1978.

**235** Thompson, J. M. *Robespierre*, Oxford: Blackwell, 1935; new one-vol. ed. 1988.

**236** Rudé, G. *Robespierre*, Collins, 1975.

**237** Hampson, N. *The Life and Opinions of Maximilian Robespierre*, Duckworth, 1974.

**238** 'Robespierre' special number of *AHRF*, 1958.

**239** Carr, J. L. *Robespierre*, Constable, 1972.

**240** Hampson, N. 'Saint-Just', ch. 12 of **86** above.

**241** Gottschalk, L. *Jean-Paul Marat*, Chicago: Chicago U.P., 1927.

**242** Gershoy, L. *Bertrand Barère*, Princeton, N.J.: Princeton U.P., 1962.

**243** Reinhard, M. *Le Grand Carnot*, 2 vols, Paris; P.U.F., 1950, 1952.

*For the effects of the Revolution on the nobility, see* **76** *and* **77** *above and:*

**244** Forster, R. 'The survival of the nobility during the French Revolution', *Past and Present*, 37, 1967.

**245** Higgonet, P. *Class, Ideology and the Rights of Nobles during the French Revolution*, Oxford: Oxford U.P., 1981.

*For the effects of the Revolution on the poor, see:*

**246** Hufton, O. *The Poor of Eighteenth Century France*, Oxford: Oxford U.P., 1974.

**247** Forrest, A. 'The conditions of the poor in Revolutionary Bordeaux', *Past and Present*, 59, 1973.

**248** Forrest, A. *The French Revolution and the Poor*, Oxford: Blackwell, 1981.

**249** Jones, C. *Charity and 'Bienfaisance': the treatment of the poor in the Montpellier region 1740–1815*, Cambridge: Cambridge U.P., 1982.

**250** Norberg, K. *Rich and Poor in Grenoble 1610–1814*, Berkeley: California U.P., 1985.

*See also:*

**251** Bruguière, M. *Gestionnaires et profiteurs de la Révolution*, Paris: Orban, 1987.

**252** Sédillot, R. *Le Coût de la Révolution française*, Paris: Perrin, 1987.

**253** Ford, F. L. 'The Revolutionary and Napoleonic Eras: how much of a watershed?', *American Historical Review*, lxix, 1963.

**254** Talmon, J. L. *The Origins of Totalitarian Democracy*, Secker & Warburg, 1952.

**255** Brécy, R. 'La Chanson révolutionnaire de 1789 à 1799', *AHRF*, 1981.

**256** Cobb, Richard and Hampson, Norman, 'The Crisis of 1789–94' and 'Personalities and Effects'. Taped discussion. Sussex Tapes, No. HE12. Sussex Publications Ltd., Freepost, Devizes, Wiltshire, SN10 1BR.

**257** Comninel, G. *Rethinking the French Revolution*, Verso, 1987.

**258** Jones, P. M. *The Peasantry in the French Revolution*, Cambridge: Cambridge U.P., 1988.

**259** Lucas, C. ed. *The Political Culture of the French Revolution*, Oxford: Pergamon Press, 1988.

**260** Best, G. ed. *The Permanent Revolution: the French Revolution and its Legacy 1789–1989*, Fontana, 1988.

**261** Harris, R. D. *Necker and the Revolution of 1789*, New York: University Press of America, 1986.

**262** Kates, G. *The Cercle Social: the Girondins and the French Revolution*, Princeton, N.J: Princeton U.P., 1985.

**263** Mason, H. T. and Doyle, W. eds. *The Impact of the French Revolution on European Consciousness*, Gloucester: Alan Sutton, 1989.

**264** Schama, S. *Citizens. A Chronicle of the French Revolution*, Viking Press, 1989.

**265** Doyle, W. *The Oxford History of the French Revolution*, Oxford: Oxford U.P., 1989.

**266** Jones, C. *The Longman Companion to the French Revolution*, Longman, 1989.

**267** Chaunu, P. *Le Grand Déclassement*, Paris: Robert Laffont, 1989.

**268** Marand-Fouquet, C. *La Femme au Temps de la Révolution*, Paris: Stock, 1988.

**269** *The French Revolution: the story so far*, Channel 4 Television, 1989.

**270** Hampson, N. 'What Difference did the French Revolution Make?', *History*, 241, June 1989.

**271** Hobsbawm, E. J. *Echoes of the Marseillaise: Two Centuries Look Back on the French Revolution*, Verso, 1990.

# Index